Inside Copilot

Inside Copilot is designed to teach users to master Copilot, Microsoft's generative AI assistant. Learn prompt engineering and use cases for Copilot in many Microsoft products at beginner, intermediate, and expert levels. Perfect for any professionals who find their schedules packed with repetitive computer tasks, Copilot can automatically generate PowerPoint presentations, draft emails on Outlook, write code on GitHub, and more. Both companies and individuals can learn to utilize Copilot to significantly speed up processes and gain an advantage.

More information about this series at `https://link.springer.com/bookseries/17432`.

Microsoft Copilot for Windows 11

Understanding the AI-Powered Features in Windows 11

Anand Narayanaswamy

Apress®

Microsoft Copilot for Windows 11: Understanding the AI-Powered Features in Windows 11

Anand Narayanaswamy
Thiruvananthapuram, Kerala, India

ISBN-13 (pbk): 979-8-8688-0582-0 ISBN-13 (electronic): 979-8-8688-0583-7
https://doi.org/10.1007/979-8-8688-0583-7

Managing Director, Apress Media LLC: Welmoed Spahr
Acquisitions Editor: Smriti Srivastava
Development Editor: Laura Berendson
Coordinating Editor: Kripa Joseph

Cover image designed by eStudioCalamar

Distributed to the book trade worldwide by Apress Media, LLC, 1 New York Plaza, New York, NY 10004, U.S.A. Phone 1-800-SPRINGER, fax (201) 348-4505, e-mail orders-ny@springer-sbm.com, or visit www.springeronline.com. Apress Media, LLC is a California LLC and the sole member (owner) is Springer Science + Business Media Finance Inc (SSBM Finance Inc). SSBM Finance Inc is a **Delaware** corporation.

For information on translations, please e-mail booktranslations@springernature.com; for reprint, paperback, or audio rights, please e-mail bookpermissions@springernature.com.

Apress titles may be purchased in bulk for academic, corporate, or promotional use. eBook versions and licenses are also available for most titles. For more information, reference our Print and eBook Bulk Sales web page at http://www.apress.com/bulk-sales.

Any source code or other supplementary material referenced by the author in this book is available to readers on GitHub (https://github.com/Apress). For more detailed information, please visit https://www.apress.com/gp/services/source-code.

If disposing of this product, please recycle the paper

Table of Contents

About the Author

 **Anand Narayanaswamy** works as an author, reviewer, and blogger based in Thiruvananthapuram, Kerala, India. He was recognized as a Microsoft MVP from 2002 to 2011 and Windows Insider MVP from 2019 to 2023 and is currently a Microsoft MVP in Windows and Devices. Anand contributes articles to leading online and print publications. He runs his blogs (netans.com and surfacebuzzer.com) and actively helps the Windows community on Quora. In his spare time, Anand loves to dig old gadgets like Microsoft Zune, iPod, and iPod Classic. He can be reached via https://twitter.com/visualanand, www.instagram.com/netanstech, and www.linkedin.com/in/anandnswamy.

Acknowledgments

Firstly, I would like to thank God for giving me the strength and energy to work. Thanks to my father, mother, and brother for their support and encouragement. I would like to thank Smriti Srivastava for all the help and assistance throughout the project. She motivated me to write the book and also shared useful tips. I thank Nirmal Selvaraj, Kripa Joseph, Linthaa Muralidharan, and the whole Apress team who worked behind this book. I highly appreciate the efforts of Sumit Dhiman who played a valuable role by providing feedback and suggestions. His comments helped to improve the quality of the content. The whole project was a great learning experience and I enjoyed the ride.

Introduction

AI has taken over the world by storm. Microsoft took the plunge by entering into the AI market with the launch of Bing Chat in February 2023. Even though Microsoft initially integrated AI chat into Bing, the subsequent months saw rapid developments with great improvements. This includes the relaxation of daily limits and the integration of Bing Chat in Microsoft Edge and Skype. Microsoft took the entire tech community by surprise by renaming Bing Chat as Microsoft Copilot in September 2023. Microsoft quickly replaced all instances of Bing Chat as Copilot with a new logo. Microsoft adopted the changes in war footing mode including the launch of Copilot Pro. Currently, Microsoft Copilot can be accessed via Windows 11, Edge, Bing, Skype, Microsoft 365, and over the Web. Moreover, Copilot is also available as a separate app via the Microsoft Store in addition to Android and iOS mobile apps. Microsoft ventured into AI image creation with Bing Image Creator, which is currently Image Creator.

Microsoft Copilot for Windows 11 kicks off with a brief overview of Generative AI and then delves deep into the evolution of Microsoft Copilot. The remaining chapters thoroughly examine the steps required to work with Microsoft Copilot in various ways including Microsoft 365. The author delves deep into the concepts with the help of concise explanations and companion screenshots. Do you want to generate AI images? We've got you covered. The book provides a comprehensive coverage of Microsoft Designer, which is used to create stunning visuals for all occasions in addition to advanced tasks. The book also covers the latest trending technologies like the Copilot key and Copilot+ PCs. Moreover, the facts enclosed inside notes in between the content amplify your Copilot learning experience. The book also includes a compact glossary related to AI and Copilot. You just need to sit before your PC and follow the instructions.

The author has adopted a lucid writing style to make sure that beginners can grasp the content quickly. Moreover, the book will be an ideal companion for students who would like to learn about Microsoft Copilot. Naturally, senior citizens won't be able to understand the usage and benefits of Copilot unless we teach them. With the help of this book, they will be able to sit and learn themselves without any assistance. The book has been written in such a way that even a school-going kid can easily master the usage of Microsoft Copilot in Windows 11. You can impress your friends by showcasing your Copilot skills.

The purpose of this book is to educate people about the features and usage of Microsoft Copilot in addition to the latest advancements under a single umbrella. After reading the book, you will be able to work with Microsoft Copilot features in Windows 11 and make the most of it with confidence.

What This Book Covers

Chapter 1: Evolution of Microsoft Copilot provides a short introduction to Generative AI followed by the various phases of Microsoft Copilot and associated products.

Chapter 2: Working with Copilot in Windows 11 – Part 1 helps you learn the steps that are required to work with Microsoft Copilot using Windows 11 search.

Chapter 3: Working with Copilot in Windows 11 – Part 2 examines the working of Copilot via the Windows 11 Taskbar. You will learn the required steps to complete various tasks using Copilot easily.

Chapter 4: Working with Copilot Using Microsoft Edge enables you to learn steps to work with Copilot using the Microsoft Edge browser.

Chapter 5: Working with Copilot Using Bing examines the usage of Copilot from within Bing, which is a popular search engine from Microsoft.

Chapter 6: Working with Copilot Using Skype provides coverage of the usage of Copilot from within the popular messaging app.

Chapter 7: Working with Copilot Web delves deep into the functioning of the Copilot web dashboard. The topics related to GPTs and plugins have been covered in detail.

Chapter 8: Working with Image Creator – Do you want to create stunning AI images? This chapter is here to your rescue.

Chapter 9: Working with Microsoft Designer provides a comprehensive coverage of the Designer tool using which you can create your AI-enabled properties.

Chapter 10: Using Copilot in Microsoft 365 examines the usage of Copilot in Microsoft 365 apps such as Word, Excel, and PowerPoint.

Chapter 11: Learning Microsoft Copilot with Windows App examines the usage of the Copilot desktop app in detail.

Chapter 12: Devices with Copilot Key enables you to know about the features and list of devices with the Copilot key.

Chapter 13: Introducing Copilot+ PCs provides a list of devices tagged as Copilot+ PCs.

Appendix A: Glossary – You will learn important terms associated with AI and Copilot.

Appendix B: Additional resources – You can update yourself about Microsoft Copilot by navigating to the mentioned resources.

What You Will Learn

- Various ways of working with Copilot in Windows 11

- GPTs and plugins in Microsoft Copilot

- Benefits of Copilot Pro

- Copilot in Microsoft 365

- Image Creator and Microsoft Designer

- Copilot key and Copilot+ PCs

System Requirements

You require a PC/laptop running Windows 11 to follow the contents included in this book. However, you can work with Copilot Web, Image Creator, and Microsoft Designer using macOS. You need Internet connectivity to work with Microsoft Copilot.

The availability of Microsoft Copilot depends upon the region. However, you can access Copilot Web and Copilot Windows apps irrespective of the region. Copilot in Windows (preview) is currently available in North America, the UK, India, parts of Asia, and South America.

Disclaimer

This book contains images that are generated via Microsoft Copilot, Image Creator, and Microsoft Designer. The AI-enabled images are only used for the sake of explanation and educational purposes. The images have no relationship with any existing humans and properties.

CHAPTER 1

Evolution of Microsoft Copilot

Generative AI, also called GenAI, is capable of generating content, images, and videos with the help of GPT/non-GPT models. The technology works when a user provides the required query, also called a prompt. Initially, Generative AI–based systems were used to create content like articles, but now the platform is also used to create images, videos, and even audio. Even though this book focuses on Microsoft Copilot, it's essential to understand the basics of Generative AI and related technologies. This chapter provides a short introduction to Generative AI followed by the evolution of Microsoft Copilot in detail.

Introducing Generative AI

Generative AI models work by learning the patterns and training data structure. The system generates new data based on similar features. The spike in the Generative AI chatbots during the late 2020s is mainly due to the improvements in transformer-enabled deep neural networks such as Large Language Models (LLMs). These chatbots comprise ChatGPT, Microsoft Copilot and Google Gemini, LLaMA, and image generation platforms like Midjourney. Generative AI can be leveraged by several industries such as software, healthcare, entertainment, finance, sales, marketing, content writing, fashion, and much more.

© Anand Narayanaswamy 2024
A. Narayanaswamy, *Microsoft Copilot for Windows 11*, Inside Copilot,
https://doi.org/10.1007/979-8-8688-0583-7_1

It all started at Dartmouth College in 1956 where the academic department of artificial intelligence (AI) was established during the sidelines of a research workshop. The researchers have seen several advancements in AI after that. However, they have raised suspicion about the nature of so-called artificial elements. The main query was whether the technology would be able to beat human intelligence. The cost involved in the development of AI is high because powerful machines are required to store data and commands. The Dartmouth Summer Research Project on AI took a clarion call for AI research, and this step has changed the scenario. Ever since the introduction of AI, artists have been making use of AI to create artistic works. In 1970, Harold Cohen created and exhibited Generative AI works created by the AARON programming language. Cohen developed AARON to generate paintings.

Technology Background

The deep learning technologies related to AI emerged during the late 2000s. These include natural language processing, image classification, speech recognition, and other related tasks. The neural networks were trained as discriminative models because of the difficulty in generative modeling. The variational autoencoder and generative adversarial network technologies produced the first deep neural networks capable of learning generative models in 2014. The discriminative models are said to be a major advancement in the field of AI and Machine Learning. These models are algorithms that are developed to not only learn the various classes but also categories in a dataset. A classic example of a discriminative model is Support Vector Machine (SVM), which is widely used for classification tasks.

The transformer network enabled advancements in Generative AI models in 2017. Previously, Long Short-Term Memory models were used that were not effective. The end result was the emergence of the first iteration of the generative pre-trained transformer (GPT-1) in 2018. This discovery has set the road map for future advancements. The GPT-2 launched in 2019 provided an ability to generalize several unsupervised tasks as a basic foundation model. The advanced imaging model named DALL·E was introduced in 2021 as a transformer-based pixel generative model. Microsoft integrated the DALL·E model into Copilot after testing the technology successfully with the original Bing Chat. Moreover, Copilot has been aggressively integrated into Microsoft Designer using which you can create stunning images, wallpapers, greeting cards, stickers, avatars, emojis, cliparts and much more.

The launch of Midjourney and Leonardo has set new dimensions to the advanced AI-based image generation from natural language prompts. OpenAI released GPT-4 in March 2023, which was regarded as an incomplete version of an artificial general intelligence (AGI) system by Microsoft. The company recently released GPT-4o, which is capable of generating images and videos. Meta also announced AI integration with WhatsApp and Instagram but is available only in select regions.

While unimodal Generative AI systems accept one type of input, multimodal systems are capable of accepting multiple types of input. For instance, GPT-4 accepts both text and image inputs. With Microsoft Copilot, you can provide prompts either as text or images. Copilot also provides the ability to scrape through an active PDF file. You can ask Copilot to generate a suitable title or seek additional information about the image using a suitable prompt.

Generative AI systems are trained on words that are modified to tokens, which LLMs can access. Some of the popular LLMs are GPT-3, GPT-4, GPT-4o, LaMDA, LLaMA, Gemini, Meta AI, and Grok. These technologies are capable of performing natural language processing and generation including machine translation. They make use of datasets via Wikipedia. Moreover, LLMs are also trained based on publicly available massive indexed data on search.

GPT models are aggressively trained in several programming languages such as HTML, C++, C#, Visual Basic, and Java in addition to older languages like COBOL, PASCAL, FORTRAN, and others. AI chatbots like Microsoft Copilot and Google Gemini generate source code based on the required command. Generative AI platforms are capable of generating stunning images and are trained via Imagen, DALL·E, Midjourney, and Stable Diffusion, among others. You can create images using lengthy prompts with the help of Microsoft Copilot.

The Generative AI technology can generate audio by leveraging natural speech synthesis and text-to-speech (TTS) capabilities. Third-party AI tools such as ElevenLabs, MusicLM, and MusicGen have the required capability to produce audio from the text prompt. You can use Microsoft Copilot to create songs based on the provided prompt. In addition to audio, you can use third-party tools such as FlexClip and Veed to create videos based on the input. You should note that the produced video won't be accurate because of the nature of the AI technology. Nowadays, researchers are aggressively using Generative AI by training them in robotics. Even medical professionals have been employing AI. Google has been involved in the development of UniPi and RT-2 multimodal vision-language-action models that can change the way we work with robots.

Generative AI models are used in several popular chatbot tools such as ChatGPT, Microsoft Copilot, GitHub Copilot, Google Gemini, Meta AI via LLaMA, Midjourney, and Stable Diffusion. The features are also integrated with Microsoft 365, which enables enterprise companies to leverage the benefits of Copilot.

Generative AI has the potential to create new content such as text, code, images, and videos with the help of AI models. With the help of AI, you can automate code generation/completion and suggestions. Microsoft has integrated GitHub Copilot into Visual Studio, which will minimize the time involved in programming. AI can be used to enhance code quality, bug checking, and other critical vulnerabilities. You can make use of GenAI chatbots like Microsoft Copilot to rewrite old source code as per the latest coding standards. Moreover, you can use AI for creating unit and integration tests. The possibilities are endless with AI, and the technology world will shake aggressively in the upcoming months.

Regulations

Generative AI technology comes with several restrictions. In recent times, there have been serious concerns about the misuse of Generative AI tools for cybercrimes, including fake news and deepfakes. It's to be noted that companies can't release AI software products without adhering to the laws of the country. You should note that companies like OpenAI, Google, and Meta have signed an agreement with the US government in July 2023. The purpose of this agreement is to watermark AI-enabled content. The US Executive Order 14110 signed in October 2023 stipulates all companies based in the United States to report while training large AI models. This move was done after amending the Defense Production Act. The Artificial Intelligence Act drafted by the European Union mandates disclosure of copyrighted material used for training Generative AI chatbots. Moreover, companies should specifically label the AI-generated response.

Sometimes, Generative AI chatbots act in a biased manner, forcing companies to take corrective steps. Google recently apologized after Gemini threw inaccuracies in historical image generation depictions. The company was also forced to disable image generation with faces because of inconsistent rendering. The recent social media outage over Meta AI rendering responses in a biased format is a classic example of AI behavior. The respective companies should invest additional time to eradicate bias from the output. It's to be noted that several newspaper companies have sued OpenAI and Microsoft because of copyright infringements.

There are also reports that the UK is also moving ahead to regulate AI after the AI Safety Summit held at Bletchley Park in November 2023. The participants expressed deep anguish over the risks and harms due to misuse of data. The Interim Measures for the Management of Generative AI Services is formed to regulate any user-specific Generative AI in China. The Cyberspace Administration of China intends to create a secure AI environment. This includes watermarking generated images and videos, including restrictions on personal data collection. Interestingly, Generative AI chatbots like ChatGPT and Google Gemini are banned in China because of safety concerns.

Even though India hasn't passed any laws to regulate AI, the government has made it clear that violations will be dealt with strictly as per the existing IT laws. OpenAI, the company behind the development of ChatGPT, recently revealed how an Israeli-based company used its platform to influence the Indian general elections held in 2024 in the form of comments, tweets, and articles. There are concerns about Generative AI replacing human jobs because the systems can quickly generate and rewrite content easily.

Imparting Proper Training

Generative AI tools such as ChatGPT, Copilot, and Gemini are trained on large and publicly available datasets. These include works that are copyrighted. That's why chatbots reveal the source from where the content is fetched below each response. For example, Copilot displays the relevant source(s) after the display of the output. There were instances where AI-based image generators produced images that were identical to the copyrighted images. Google recently discontinued the generation of images with human faces in Gemini after a series of complaints regarding the generated images. Getty Images has sued Stability AI because of the usage of its images to train Stable Diffusion. The Authors Guild and *The New York Times* have also filed lawsuits against Microsoft and OpenAI over the usage of their articles and blogs to train Copilot and ChatGPT.

Evolution of GPTs

Generative pre-trained transformer (GPT) is a popular Large Language Model (LLM) that is employed in the Generative AI tools such as ChatGPT, Copilot, and Gemini. OpenAI is the company behind the development of GPTs. They are used in natural language processing tasks via artificial neural networks. GPTs are trained on language datasets of text that can generate quality content based on the relevant query, which is otherwise called a prompt.

The evolution of GPT dates back to 2018 with the launch of the first iteration, which is named GPT-1. The model comprised a 12-level and 12-headed transformer decoder followed by linear softmax. The initial version of GPT-2 was launched on February 14, 2019, with modified normalization and 1.5 billion parameter count followed by the full version on November 5, 2019.

The higher scalable GPT-3 based on GPT-2 was launched on May 28, 2020, with 175 billion parameter count followed by GPT-3.5 on March 15, 2022. Microsoft initially launched Copilot based on the GPT-3 model and subsequently switched over to GPT-4.

The advanced GPT-4 with 1.7 trillion parameter count was released on March 14, 2023, with support for both text and images as input. OpenAI launched GPT-4 Turbo in November 2023 as a multimodal model capable of processing both text and image inputs. The model is packed with extensive data, which is capable of providing accurate current information.

OpenAI announced the release of GPT-4o, also called GPT-4 Omni, on May 13, 2024, with support for text, image, and audio prompts. GPT-4o is available for ChatGPT free users in limited access mode in addition to the GPT-4o mini model. Meanwhile, ChatGPT Plus subscribers have access to GPT-4o, GPT-4o mini, GPT-4 models with support for advanced data analysis and DALL·E image generation.

Note   Microsoft recently announced that GPT-4o will be integrated into Copilot in the upcoming future. The team also demonstrated the capabilities by using the *Minecraft* game with the GPT-4o model.

OpenAI is expected to release GPT-5 by Q4 2025 with PhD-level intelligence. The upcoming model will be developed to achieve human-level performance with advanced memory and reasoning functionalities. Microsoft revealed the latest version of its Small Language Model (SLM) named Phi-3.5 on August 20, 2024. The AI models and related technologies are under continuous development. You can expect the launch of several new AI models and chatbots regularly, as the field is evolving rapidly. The future is bright for AI, and it's up to you to use it responsibly.

Evolution of Chatbots

OpenAI's ChatGPT leverages its own GPT model to generate responses. The free version provides support for GPT-3.5 with limited access to GPT-4o, file uploads, custom GPTs, and much more. Microsoft borrowed OpenAI's GPT language model and integrated it with Copilot, which is available in Windows 11, Microsoft Edge, Skype, and the Web. The company also released a Copilot Windows app that can be pinned to the Taskbar, including access via Windows 11 desktop and Start menu. Microsoft also launched an exclusive graphics app named Microsoft Designer based on Generative AI. Google's Gemini AI has been integrated with the language model named PaLM. This model has been designed, developed, and trained by Google and accepts both text and image prompts.

Meta also released its own LLM named LLaMA with Facebook, WhatsApp, and Instagram integration. The access is limited to certain countries. However, Meta AI is currently available on WhatsApp in India. X (formerly Twitter) also released an exclusive Generative AI model named Grok. LumaLabs recently launched Dream Machine, which is a Generative

AI model for the creation of high-quality videos from text and images. The service is available for free with a limit of five shots per day with an enhanced limit for paid users. Imagine you are interacting with ChatGPT, Copilot, or Gemini. This means that you are communicating with chatbots. Table 1-1 provides a quick glance of the evolution of the popular chatbots.

Table 1-1. *Learn the Evolution of Generative AI Chatbots*

Chatbot	Company	Launch Date	Technologies	URL
ChatGPT	OpenAI	Nov 30, 2022	GPT-3.5/4/Turbo/ 4o/4o mini	chatgpt.com
Bing Chat	Microsoft	Feb 7, 2023	GPT-3/4	Renamed as Copilot
Copilot	Microsoft	Sep 21, 2023	GPT-4/Turbo/GPT-4o	copilot.microsoft.com
Bard	Google	March 21, 2023	PaLM 2	Renamed as Gemini
Gemini	Google	Feb 20, 2024	Gemini	gemini.google.com
Grok	X	Nov 4, 2023	Python/Rust	x.com

Evolution of Microsoft Copilot

We all worked even before the launch of Microsoft Copilot, which is a Generative AI chatbot. We worked aggressively during the pandemic times even without Copilot. We never heard about technologies such as ChatGPT, Copilot, Gemini, and Gork during those times. Let's trace back as to how we worked. We often open a web browser such as Microsoft Edge or Google Chrome and navigate to search engines like Bing, Google, Yahoo, and much more. If you had worked online during the late 1990s, you would have worked with Yahoo, Lycos, and Altavista search engines. The process works like this: you input a query into the search box, and the relevant search engine throws the result. Let's check in Figure 1-1 as to how the result of a traditional search engine appears on your desktop.

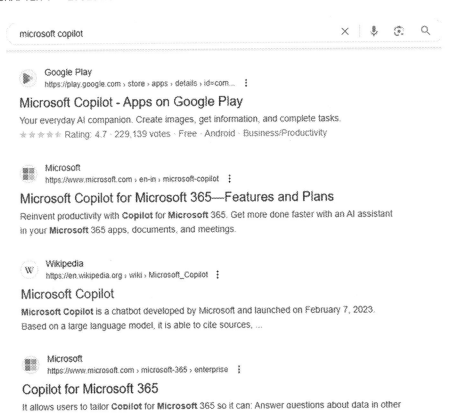

Figure 1-1. *This is how a traditional non-AI search engine displays the result*

As you can see, the search engine provides the results with the title, description, and URL. You have to manually visit each search result, and the whole process should be repeated until you find a specific answer relevant to your query. The search results rendered through web browsers are paginated. This means you have to select each page manually to locate the relevant information. Sometimes, you will have to select several pages and then manually click the links to locate a piece of specific information. You only had search engines at your disposal. It's still a credible tool because the system provides links from reputed sources that are ranked according to the popularity of the domain. You just need to open the link and read the content, which will be supported by images and videos. You can also select the internal links from the displayed web pages to locate additional resources.

Even though Microsoft's Bing exists, Google dominates the search engine space because publishers often produce content in such a way as to rank them better on Google only. Sometimes, web pages rank higher on Bing than Google. It all depends upon the algorithm adopted by the search engines. Both Google and Microsoft keep on changing the algorithm that affects the display of your content. Google's Panda update was notorious because web pages ranked higher before the rollout of the update drastically went down in the overall search rankings. This will not only affect the traffic but also the overall revenue of publishers.

History

Microsoft established a strategic partnership with OpenAI in 2019 and started to infuse funds. As part of the deal, OpenAI systems are being run on the Microsoft Azure cloud platform. Microsoft revealed in September 2020 that it had licensed OpenAI's GPT-3 technology. Even though other users can receive output from its public API, Microsoft will only have access to the underlying language model. OpenAI created an Internet sensation in November 2022 with the launch of GPT-3-enabled ChatGPT chatbot. The system was primarily designed to deliver information based on prompts. The whole system gained worldwide attention with users storming into ChatGPT. A major development happened on January 23, 2023, when Microsoft announced a $10 billion investment in OpenAI.

Origin of Bing Chat

Just days after the massive investment in OpenAI, Microsoft Copilot (originally named Bing Chat) was launched on February 7, 2023. Bing Chat was designed based on the GPT-3 language model but was upgraded to the

GPT-4 language model. The system generated answers based on queries by citing sources. Bing Chat was able to deliver short/long essays based on the tone, create poems, perform calculations, and much more. Microsoft renamed Bing Chat as Copilot in late 2023 to provide uniformity across Microsoft AI products like GitHub Copilot.

Microsoft continues to add new features and capabilities to Copilot. The chatbot was expanded with support for plugins. For example, Microsoft Copilot provides the capability to generate songs via the Suno AI plugin. Copilot can be considered as an advanced replacement for Cortana, which has been discontinued by Microsoft.

Bing Chat was initially launched as an integrated feature for the Bing web browser and Microsoft Edge. Microsoft embedded Copilot into Windows 11 during the sidelines of the Microsoft Build conference. You can easily launch Copilot in Windows 11 directly from the Taskbar. Microsoft announced the addition of a dedicated Copilot key for Windows devices in January 2024. This is a major development in the quest to tag Windows 11 devices as AI enabled.

Even though Microsoft Copilot was launched based on the GPT-3 model, the system currently makes use of the GPT-4 language model based on Microsoft Prometheus. Copilot Pro subscribers have access to the advanced GPT-4 Turbo model. The system has been fine-tuned with not only supervised but also reinforcement learning techniques. The Microsoft Copilot dashboard looks similar to ChatGPT, but you can specify the output tone. Moreover, Copilot displays sources from where the output is being fetched. The interactions with Copilot are saved just like ChatGPT. Microsoft Copilot is designed in such a way that it can communicate with numerous languages and dialects.

The Bing AI chatbot was initially made available in waitlist mode to users of Microsoft Edge and Bing mobile apps. Microsoft revealed that one million people joined the Bing Chat waitlist within 48 hours of the official launch. The Bing Chat UI looked as shown in Figure 1-2.

Figure 1-2. *Bing Chat user interface*

Microsoft restricted the chat session to 5 with a limit of 50 queries per day per user. The company relaxed the restrictions to 30 chat sessions and 300 queries per day. These restrictions helped the company to balance the server load and also to provide quick replies. Microsoft eliminated the waitlist requirement and migrated the AI chatbot to Open Preview on May 4, 2023. Bing Chat was made available for consumption on non-Edge web browsers such as Google Chrome, Firefox, and others on August 4, 2023. Microsoft Copilot is available for free just like search engines. With the help of the free version, you can access several features including the ability to create songs and images. The image creation does come up with restrictions in the form of tokens for Copilot Free users, while the Pro subscribers have 100 tokens per day. The system generates images via OpenAI's DALL·E technology using powerful algorithms.

Image Creator

Microsoft released Bing Image Creator (currently Image Creator) powered by OpenAI's DALL·E 2 technology in March 2023. The system was designed to generate rich and compelling images based on the provided prompt.

13

The image creator tool was upgraded with DALL·E 3 in October 2023. Like with all other AI image generation tools, Microsoft has applied filters to prevent the generation of offensive images. Microsoft recently renamed Bing Image Creator to Image Creator using which you can create amazing images. It's the same as the original Image Creator except for the change in the name. The dashboard of the Image Creator looks as shown in Figure 1-3.

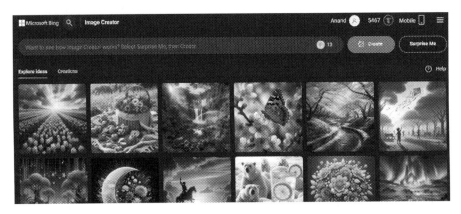

Figure 1-3. *Create stunning images with Image Creator*

You should note that the screenshot is the home page of the Microsoft Image Creator. The thumbnails have no relation with living characters or humans. Microsoft also launched a complete Designer app using which you can create images, stickers, and designs as well as erase selected content from existing images. The app also includes several modules for performing tasks such as greeting card creation, background removal, restyling images, and much more.

Note   Do you want to learn Microsoft Designer in detail? Refer to Chapter 9.

Microsoft 365 Copilot

Microsoft announced the launch of Microsoft 365 Copilot on March 16, 2023. The main purpose is to provide Copilot as a value-added feature to Microsoft 365 with special emphasis on business productivity. Microsoft 365 Copilot is oriented for enterprise companies who would like to have a secured AI interaction. Moreover, companies will be able to experience Enterprise-grade data protection with Microsoft Graph grounding. The team members will be able to customize and extend via Microsoft Copilot Studio. As of this writing, Microsoft 365 Copilot costs $30 per user/month with an option for an annual subscription. The prices are subject to change without any notification. You need access to a Microsoft 365 Personal or Family subscription to work with Microsoft 365 Copilot. With the help of Microsoft 365 Copilot, you can automate Word, Excel, PowerPoint, OneNote, and Outlook, including Microsoft Teams. For example, you can ask Copilot after logging in to Microsoft 365 Word app to compose an article, poem, letter, or listicle. Copilot in PowerPoint enables you to create stunning presentations filled with quality content and images. You can also ask Copilot to fetch specific information related to the active PDF document that has been opened on the web browser. The Copilot with Commercial data protection is available on Android and iOS mobile platforms via Microsoft Copilot, Microsoft 365, Microsoft Start, and Bing apps, respectively. However, you need to sign in to the app using work or school (Entra ID) accounts.

Note You can subscribe to Copilot Pro to work with Copilot using Microsoft 365. You can also create documents in Microsoft 365 for free via OneDrive to work with Copilot.

Copilot in Word

With the help of Copilot in Word, you can create, rewrite, and summarize your documents to the next level. You can also transform text into a table automatically. Copilot can also discover information from your document irrespective of the page count. For instance, you can load and ask Copilot in Word to summarize the content. You can also use the chatbot to write articles, blog posts, letters, poems, and much more.

Copilot in Excel

The integration of Copilot in Excel is considered a big step in the exploration of data. You will find Copilot useful to drill down lengthy spreadsheets to locate relevant information. The Copilot support in Excel will be useful for large hypermarkets and enterprise companies since these organizations will have to analyze massive data of both consumers and suppliers. You can highlight, filter, and sort data with Copilot support from within Excel. The main prerequisite is that the Excel data should be active on OneDrive and must be in a tabular format.

Copilot in PowerPoint

You can easily create powerful and impressive presentations via Copilot in PowerPoint. You just need to provide the relevant prompt to enable PowerPoint to create the required slides. Microsoft Copilot can convert a Word document into beautiful presentations with complete content and images. Moreover, Copilot provides intelligent prompts using which you can adjust your presentations. It's possible to shorten lengthy presentations and make use of natural language commands to adjust layouts and animations. You need to provide the link to your Word file after creation/uploading to OneDrive to generate PowerPoint presentations via Copilot. However, if you would like to make use of the Word file directly, then you need to have Microsoft 365 Copilot subscription.

Copilot in Outlook

Copilot in Outlook enables you to work with emails effectively. If your inbox includes thousands of emails, then Copilot can fetch emails as per your prompt and keywords. You can ask Copilot to summarize an email with special importance to suggested action items, replies, and follow-up meetings. You can also ask Copilot to draft emails by specifying length and tone, which is also called email coaching.

Copilot in OneNote

OneNote enables you to simplify note capturing capabilities, and the integration of Copilot takes this one step further. You can ask queries via prompts in addition to the ability to generate and summarize content. Copilot enables you to get information from lengthy files quickly, which saves you a considerable amount of time.

Copilot in Teams

Microsoft Teams is an excellent collaboration tool using which you can interact with your colleagues via both text and video in a secured way. Copilot in Teams intelligently organizes and summarizes content in addition to fetching answers to queries. Copilot creates meeting agendas quickly based on chat history. You can follow up and schedule the next check-in from within Copilot. Microsoft has integrated Copilot in several other products such as Loop, Microsoft Stream, Whiteboard, Graph, Graph Connectors, and Purview.

From Copilot to Microsoft Copilot

Microsoft announced the rebranding of Copilot to Microsoft Copilot on September 21, 2023. The company introduced a new Microsoft Copilot logo as shown in Figure 1-4 as part of the major refresh. Microsoft replaced all Copilot instances with the new logo such as Copilot in Windows (preview), Windows 11 search, Bing, Skype, Web app, mobile apps as well as the newly launched Copilot Windows app.

Figure 1-4. *The Official Microsoft Copilot Logo in Action*

Windows Copilot was also launched during the sidelines of the Build 2023 conference. It was designed for Windows 11 devices using which users can directly access Copilot via an icon located on the Taskbar. However, Microsoft renamed Windows Copilot as Microsoft Copilot in October 2023. Subsequently, Microsoft Edge's Bing Chat functionality was also renamed as Copilot.

A major development happened on November 15, 2023, when Microsoft completely rebranded Bing Chat as Microsoft Copilot. Microsoft also renamed Bing Image Creator as Image Creator by Designer. Microsoft Copilot was also made generally available starting November 1, 2023, for Microsoft 365 Enterprise customers who purchase more than 300 licenses. You can also work with Microsoft Copilot using the respective Android and iOS apps.

Dedicated Copilot Key

Microsoft took tech enthusiasts by storm on January 4, 2024, with the announcement of a dedicated Copilot key for Windows 11 devices. The manufacturers have showcased Windows 11 devices with Copilot key during the sidelines of the Consumer Electronics Show (CES) and Mobile World Congress (MWC) 2024 conferences. In Figure 1-5, you can view the keyboard of the latest Microsoft Surface keyboard with the Copilot key. It's the second key to the right side of the space bar.

Figure 1-5. *The new dedicated Copilot key will boost productivity*

You can expect wide availability of Windows 11 devices with the Copilot key by the end of 2024. You just need to press the Copilot key as shown in Figure 1-5 to launch the Microsoft Copilot user interface, which will be docked to the right side of the Windows 11 desktop.

Note   You can also access Microsoft Copilot in Windows 11 by hitting the WIN+C keyboard shortcut. However, Microsoft could make changes to the key as per user feedback.

The purpose behind the introduction of a new Copilot key after 30 years of the Windows logo key is to enhance user experience and overall productivity. You can ask Copilot to open apps such as Notepad, Snipping Tool, Calculator, Settings, and much more. Moreover, you can ask Copilot to change the desktop environment from Light to Dark theme and vice versa. You should note that Microsoft reserves the right to change the functionality of Copilot.

Microsoft Copilot Pro

Microsoft launched Copilot Pro on January 15, 2024 with additional perks to enhance the overall Copilot user experience. Copilot Pro is available with enhanced features with priority access to not only GPT-4 but also GPT-4 Turbo even during peak usage periods with enhanced performance. This will enable accelerated generation of answers, content, and AI images. The bundled Copilot GPT Builder enables users to create custom Copilot chatbots. With Copilot Pro, you can access Copilot in Microsoft 365 apps such as Word, Excel, PowerPoint, and Outlook. Moreover, you can experience faster image generation with DALL·E 3 with an additional 100 daily boosts with Microsoft Designer. Copilot Pro costs $20 per month. However, you can subscribe to free trial for 30 days to test-drive the features and performance.

Note   Buy Copilot Pro: `www.microsoft.com/en-us/store/b/ copilotpro`

Windows 11

Microsoft has integrated Copilot into Windows 11 with powerful features. You will be able to work with Microsoft Copilot directly by selecting the Copilot in Windows (preview) Taskbar icon. In addition to standard search functions, you can ask Copilot in Windows to open the Calculator app by simply providing the prompt *open calculator*. You have to provide the prompt by launching the Copilot icon from the Taskbar, which is located at the right side of the Notifications icon. In the same way, you can query Copilot to open Notepad, WordPad, Snipping Tool, Paint, Settings app, and much more.

Note   WordPad was discontinued by Microsoft in September 2023. The app was released on August 24, 1995. The company recommends improved Notepad or Microsoft Word as alternatives.

You can also change the entire Windows 11 desktop to Dark mode from Light and vice versa. You have to provide a prompt like *change to dark mode* by selecting the Copilot in Windows (preview) Taskbar icon.

Copilot Apps

Microsoft Copilot is now available as a separate app from Microsoft Store. The app will be pinned to the Windows 11 Taskbar. Microsoft Copilot apps for Android and iOS can be downloaded from Google Play Store and Apple App Store. You can make use of voice to provide prompts, and Copilot will deliver results instantly. However, you should sign in with your Microsoft account to enable Copilot to generate images. You can also access Microsoft Copilot via Telegram. You should add the Copilot Official Bot from within the app and interact with the chatbot.

Copilot+ PCs

Microsoft announced the launch of Copilot+ PCs on May 20, 2024. The company revealed that it is revolutionizing the PC for the AI era with Copilot+ PCs. The new technology will be fulfilled via hybrid AI with Copilot+ PCs. Microsoft disclosed that enterprise companies can deploy Copilot+ PCs to enjoy fastest and intelligent Windows 11 PC. Copilot+ PCs leverage a neural processing unit (NPU) silicon, which is capable of delivering an incredible 40+ trillion operations per second (TOPS). The NPU is a chipset embedded inside the motherboard, which is exclusively designed to run AI tasks locally and smoothly. Moreover, organizations can experience a brilliant AI endpoint for work in addition to a foundation for your dedicated chip-to-cloud solution stack.

The main advantage of Copilot+ PCs is that they have the potential to unlock industry-compliant AI acceleration with up to 2x faster NPU performance when compared with MacBook Air and MacBook Pro. The advanced privacy module ensures that AI running on your Copilot+ PCs will never be able to access your private content. With the help of Copilot+ PCs, companies can effectively make use of Copilot for Microsoft 365, which provides powerful AI solutions at work. Copilot+ PCs will be integrated with specific modules to handle demanding workloads. They provide an intuitive AI experience with advanced Windows Security.

Copilot+ PCs are currently equipped with an advanced Qualcomm Snapdragon X Elite Arm processor. The CPU is capable of offering up to 22 hours of video playback and 15 hours of web browsing, respectively. Copilot+ PCs are specifically designed to provide a seamless user experience with business apps and Windows 365 Cloud PCs. Intel and AMD will also release advanced processors for the development of Copilot+ PCs.

Note   Microsoft revealed that Copilot+ PCs devices with Intel and AMD processors will be available within the next few months.

The devices that are shipped with Copilot+ PCs will ship with new features such as Recall, Live Captions with translation, and Windows Studio Effects. These features are designed to enhance the productivity of users irrespective of organization size. With the help of Recall, you can locate any content on your desktop just by entering the relevant search keyword. The Recall will display accurate snapshots of the most relevant content based on either the text or visual search. Moreover, Microsoft has integrated advanced privacy controls using which you can decide the information that Recall can capture.

The Live Captions integrated into Copilot+ PCs is capable of translating more than 40 languages into English. This includes speakers in real-time video calls, streamed content, and recordings. The Windows Studio Effects have been upgraded with features such as flattering portrait lighting, creative filters, and natural-looking eye contact. Moreover, the enhanced noise cancelling and background blur shut out distraction capabilities improve the way you interact with users over video.

Microsoft has established collaboration with manufacturers for the development of Copilot+ PCs. Some of the new devices that are fully compliant with Copilot+ PCs are Acer Swift 14 A, ASUS Vivobook S15, Dell XPS 13, HP OmniBook X, HP EliteBook ultra, Lenovo Yoga Slim 7X, Lenovo T14 S, Samsung Galaxy Book4 Edge, Microsoft Surface Pro, and Surface Laptop.

Summary

In this chapter, you have learned the evolution of Generative AI and Microsoft Copilot in detail. You also learned the various phases of GPT and the evolution of chatbots. This chapter also provided a short outline about Image Creator, the dedicated Copilot key, and Copilot Pro as well as the newly launched Copilot+ PCs. The upcoming chapters will delve deep into the working of Copilot in Windows 11 and image creation capabilities. The purpose of this chapter is to help you learn all the required Copilot tools and technologies that you can explore while going through this book.

CHAPTER 2

Working with Copilot in Windows 11 – Part 1

Microsoft Copilot is a Generative AI–based Large Language Model (LLM) chatbot, which is capable of generating content based on queries or prompts. Copilot also provides the ability to create lists, poems, short stories, and recipes as well as the ability to generate impressive images. The possibilities are endless, and it's up to you to decide the way to work with the Copilot. Microsoft has integrated Copilot with Windows 11, and you can work directly by selecting an icon from the Taskbar. However, there are several other ways by which you can access Copilot from within Windows 11. In this chapter, you will learn the steps required to work with Copilot via Windows 11 search.

Accessing Copilot in Windows 11

To work with Copilot, you need access to a device running Windows 11. Microsoft is rolling out Copilot in a phased manner across various regions. If Copilot is available on your Windows 11 device, you will see an icon either in the Taskbar adjacent to the search box or on the far-right side of the Taskbar adjacent to the Notifications bell icon. The Copilot icon was originally placed near the search box, but the subsequent updates shifted the icon to the right side of the Notifications bell icon as shown in Figure 2-1.

© Anand Narayanaswamy 2024
A. Narayanaswamy, *Microsoft Copilot for Windows 11*, Inside Copilot,
https://doi.org/10.1007/979-8-8688-0583-7_2

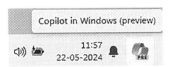

Figure 2-1. *Kick-start your Copilot Journey*

Microsoft recently released Windows 11 version 24H2 to the Windows Insiders Release Preview Channel with an evolved Copilot user experience. This means that you can access Copilot via an app that will be pinned to the Taskbar. You can easily resize, move, and snap the window just like any other app. This new update will be rolling out to Windows Insiders in the Dev, Canary, and Beta channels in the upcoming months.

Microsoft also announced the retirement of the WIN+C keyboard shortcut as part of this new user experience in Windows 11 version 24H2. The devices with a dedicated Copilot key will open the Copilot chatbot upon hitting the key. Microsoft also announced a new way to open Copilot on devices without the Copilot key. You can make use of WIN+number position for Copilot pinned to your Taskbar. However, the new changes are currently available only for Windows Insiders in the Release Preview Channel.

Note   Windows Insiders are a group of tech enthusiasts who regularly provide feedback after testing new versions. You can join the Windows Insider Program from within Windows 11 by navigating to Settings ➤ Windows Update ➤ Windows Insider Program and by selecting the *Get started* button.

Let's examine the various methods by which you can access Copilot in Windows 11. You can work with Copilot either by selecting the search box or by directly clicking the *Copilot in Windows (preview)* icon from the Windows 11 Taskbar. Additionally, you can work with Copilot after installing the app from the Microsoft Store.

In this chapter, you will learn the steps required to access Copilot via the Windows 11 search. The first step is to select the *Ask Copilot* icon located at the top-right side of the search box as shown in Figure 2-2.

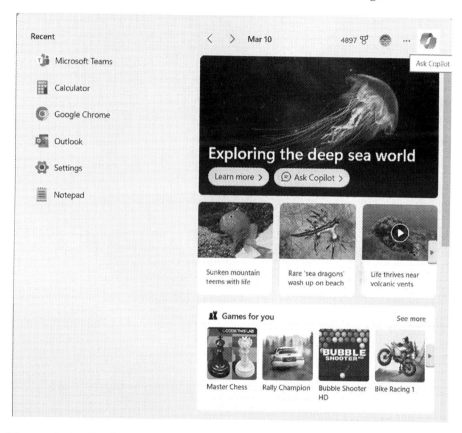

Figure 2-2. *Explore Copilot via Windows 11 search*

You will see the Copilot dashboard with relevant information as shown in Figure 2-3. The dashboard displays automated prompts that you can make use of straightaway.

Figure 2-3. *Get started with Copilot*

Note   You can also select the *Ask Copilot* button located inside the search suggestion. Copilot provides the response based on the displayed topic. If you select the *Learn more* button, the search results are displayed in Microsoft Bing.

If you select a prompt from the sliding carousel, Copilot displays the relevant response based on the selected topic. You can also provide a query, also called a prompt, which can be up to 2000 characters in length. A prompt spans across either a single line or multiple lines depending upon your requirements.

Note   You interact with Microsoft Copilot using queries. In AI parlance, queries are called prompts.

Let's select an item from the Copilot dashboard carousel, and the output looks like as displayed in Figure 2-4.

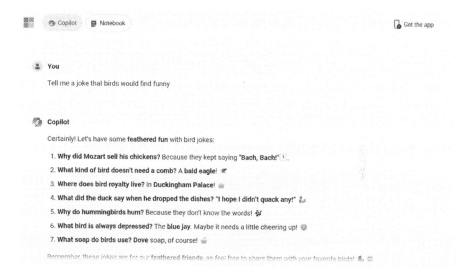

Figure 2-4. *Check out the results delivered by Copilot*

If you scroll down the Copilot dashboard, you will find the links to sources from where answers were fetched, including images with jokes, as displayed in Figure 2-5.

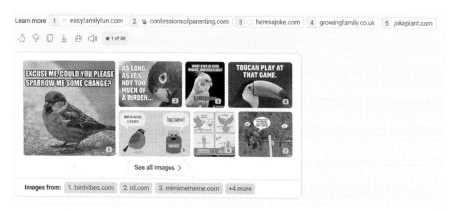

Figure 2-5. *Copilot displays sources with relevant images*

Exporting Copilot Output

You can like, dislike, and copy the generated Copilot output as well as export the content. If you select the *Export* icon located below the source link row, you will see the screen as shown in Figure 2-6.

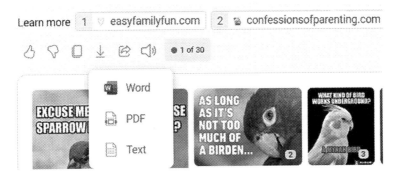

Figure 2-6. *Share Copilot results easily*

You can export the Copilot output in Word, PDF, and Text formats, respectively. In Figure 2-7, you can see the resulting screen after selecting the PDF export option.

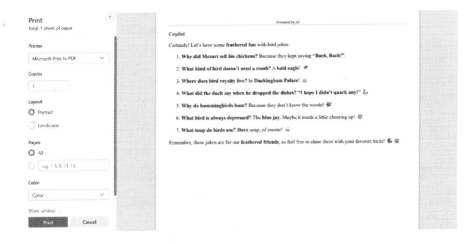

Figure 2-7. *Exporting Copilot output via PDF*

You will see the relevant output in the Print dashboard. You can easily transfer the content from Microsoft Print to PDF format by selecting the *Print* button. That's it. Your Copilot output will be saved as a separate PDF file. Your interactions with Copilot will be automatically saved inside the dashboard as shown in Figure 2-8 under the *Recents* section.

Figure 2-8. *Copilot maintains a history perfectly*

The right side also displays Copilot GPTs and the available plugins. We will examine them in detail in an upcoming chapter.

Picking a Conversation Style

Microsoft Copilot provides three conversation styles: Creative, Balanced, and Precise. The default conversation style is Balanced. Let's now provide a prompt and check out the results of the response delivered by all three conversation styles.

Note   Microsoft is currently experimenting with a new Copilot user interface without the three conversation styles. However, the styles could appear intermittently if you are using the Copilot Free version. The conversation styles are available for Copilot Pro as per our testing. Microsoft hasn't yet clarified that the styles are only reserved for Copilot Pro users. Even if you are not able to view the styles, the content discussed here holds good. Alternatively, you can select the three horizonal lines (hamburger menu), select Settings and change the Country/Region to United States - English to view the conversation styles.

Prompt: *Can you provide the name of Kerala capital?*

Style: *Creative*

In Figure 2-9, you can observe how the Creative conversation style displays the output.

You

Can you provide the name of Kerala capital?

Copilot

The capital of Kerala is **Thiruvananthapuram** [1]. It's also known by its former name, Trivandrum [2]

Figure 2-9. Copilot delivers a creative output

Prompt: *Can you provide the name of Kerala capital?*

Style: *Balanced*

The output will be rendered as follows:

Certainly! The capital of Kerala is Thiruvananthapuram (commonly shortened to TVM), formerly known as Trivandrum. It is the most populous city in Kerala, with a population of 957,730 as of 2011. Thiruvananthapuram is located on the west coast of India near the extreme south of the mainland. It is a major information technology hub in Kerala, contributing 55% of the state's software exports as of 2016. Mahatma Gandhi referred to it as the "Evergreen city of India." The city's undulating terrain features low coastal hills, and it has a rich historical background, later becoming the capital of the princely state of Travancore

Prompt: *Can you provide the name of Kerala capital?*

Style: *Precise*

The Precise style is identical to Creative but with minor modifications as shown in Figure 2-10.

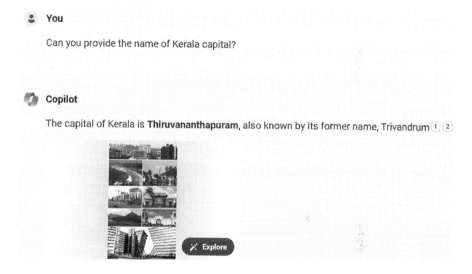

Figure 2-10. *It is the precise answer to our query*

While the Creative and Precise conversation styles emit single-line answers, the Balanced style generates longer responses. You will be able to learn additional information about Kerala's capital.

Let's examine the working of Copilot using another prompt.

Prompt: *Who founded Microsoft?*

Style: *Creative*

The prompt is simple and the response will appear as shown in Figure 2-11.

Figure 2-11. *Know about Microsoft creatively*

Prompt: *Who founded Microsoft?*

Style: *Balanced*

As you can see, the Balanced mode delivered lengthy content as in Figure 2-12.

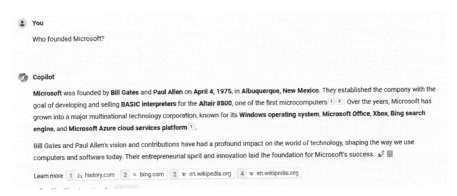

Figure 2-12. *Content delivered in Balanced mode by Copilot*

Prompt: *Who founded Microsoft?*

Style: *Precise*

In Precise style, Copilot delivers a crisp output as shown in Figure 2-13.

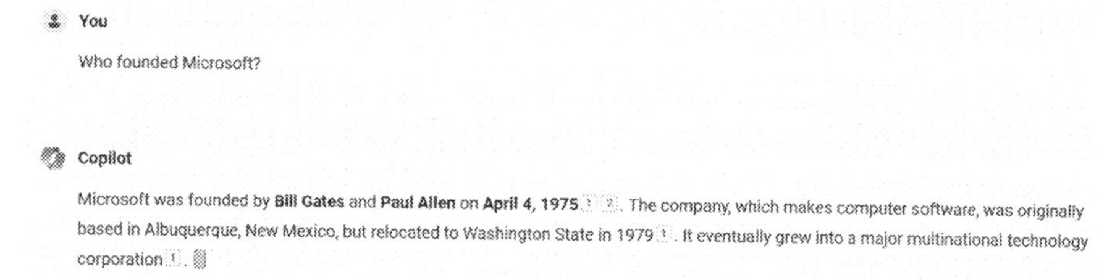

You

Who founded Microsoft?

Copilot

Microsoft was founded by **Bill Gates** and **Paul Allen** on **April 4, 1975** [1] [2]. The company, which makes computer software, was originally based in Albuquerque, New Mexico, but relocated to Washington State in 1979 [1]. It eventually grew into a major multinational technology corporation [1].

Figure 2-13. *Know about Microsoft precisely*

As you can observe, there are subtle differences in the response delivered by Copilot. It's the Balanced conversation style that provides crisp answers. You will also notice discrepancies in the ZIP code. You should always cross-check the answers if you feel something wrong because of the nature of AI. You will notice that the conversation style button changes color upon selection. While the Creative button is purple, the default Balanced button looks blue. It's green color for the Precise conversation style.

Coding via Copilot

Microsoft Copilot is capable of helping you out with your coding tasks. Copilot provides support for all major programming languages. Shall we try to run a C# code using Copilot? We asked Copilot to demonstrate the usage of arrays in C# as per the following prompt.

Note   You should note that AI prompts are not case-sensitive.

Prompt: *Write a C# code to demonstrate the usage of arrays.*

Copilot provides a brief description followed by the source code as shown in Figure 2-14.

```
C#

using System;

class Program
{
    static void Main()
    {
        // Declare and initialize an array
        int[] array = new int[5] {1, 2, 3, 4, 5};

        // Print each value of the array
        for (int i = 0; i < array.Length; i++)
        {
            Console.WriteLine("Element at index " + i + ": " + array[i]);
        }
    }
}
```

AI-generated code. Review and use carefully. More info on FAQ.

Figure 2-14. *Learn coding easily with Microsoft Copilot*

Let's now try the same programming query for the Python language. You will see the output as shown in Figure 2-15, but you have to scroll for the full explanation and the resulting source code. Copilot nicely splits every module and provides a simplified explanation.

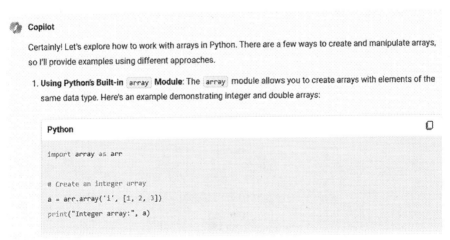

Figure 2-15. *Rock-solid Python programming with Microsoft Copilot*

Microsoft Copilot provides support for several programming languages, and this includes Ruby. Let's try the same prompt and ask Copilot to deliver the output (see Figure 2-16) as per the Ruby language.

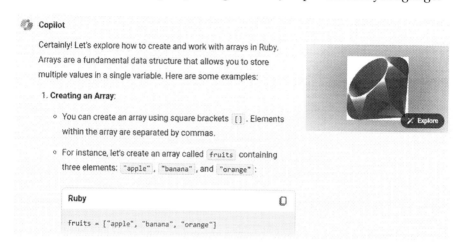

Figure 2-16. *Get Rubified with Microsoft Copilot*

Copilot divides the output into several headings as in Figure 2-16, such as array creation, accessing array elements, and much more. It's easy and fun to learn programming with Microsoft Copilot.

Let's go vintage and test how Copilot responds to COBOL programming. The prompt that was tested is *write a COBOL program to add 5 and 6*, and the resulting output looks as shown in Figure 2-17.

Copilot

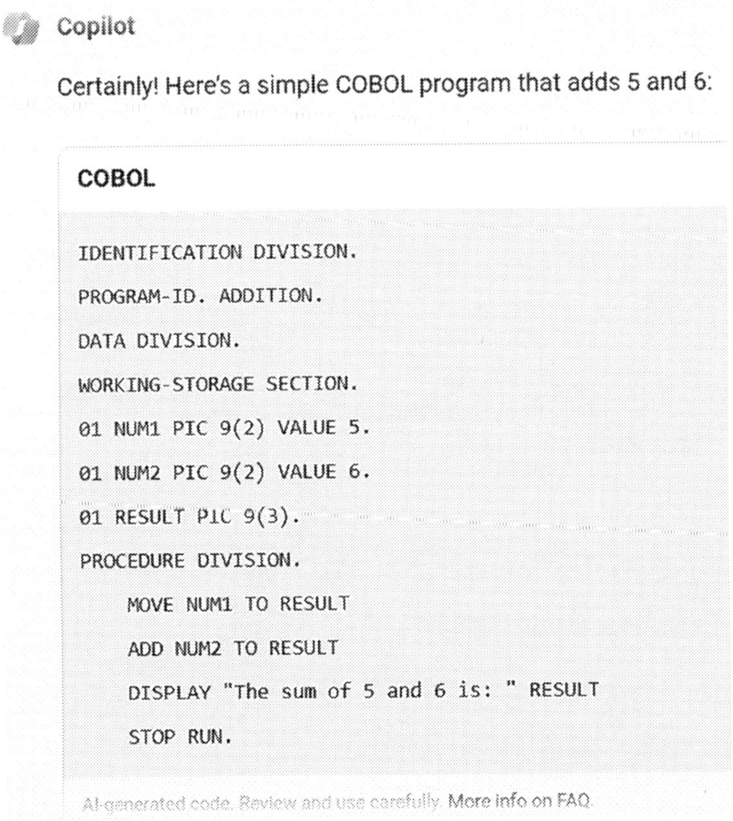

Certainly! Here's a simple COBOL program that adds 5 and 6:

COBOL

```cobol
IDENTIFICATION DIVISION.
PROGRAM-ID. ADDITION.
DATA DIVISION.
WORKING-STORAGE SECTION.
01 NUM1 PIC 9(2) VALUE 5.
01 NUM2 PIC 9(2) VALUE 6.
01 RESULT PIC 9(3).
PROCEDURE DIVISION.
    MOVE NUM1 TO RESULT
    ADD NUM2 TO RESULT
    DISPLAY "The sum of 5 and 6 is: " RESULT
    STOP RUN.
```

AI-generated code. Review and use carefully. More info on FAQ.

Figure 2-17. *Learn vintage COBOL with Copilot*

Copilot displays a disclaimer that the code is AI generated, and you have to use carefully each response. Microsoft also compiled the list of FAQs associated with Copilot, and you can access it directly by selecting the link specified below the source code. Toward the end of the code, Copilot provides a detailed bulleted explanation, which helps you to learn about the generated code. If you are a student or a prospective programmer, then you should double-check the Copilot response by directly practicing the code using the relevant programming language compiler or Integrated Development Environment (IDE) tools like Visual Studio. Moreover, students should try to learn programming traditionally and limit the usage of AI chatbots. This will help them to solve complex problems when they approach job interviews.

Refreshing Copilot

If you refresh the Copilot dashboard or select the *Ask Copilot* icon from the Windows 11 search box once again, you will see an additional set of prompts. Let's write a song that celebrates the beauty of the Earth. Microsoft Copilot automatically writes the poem with verse 1 followed by chorus, verse 2 followed by chorus, etc., as shown in Figure 2-18.

 Copilot

Sure, here's a song that celebrates the beauty of our Earth:

```
(Verse 1)
Gazing at the sky so blue,
A world of vibrant colors in view.
Mountains high and oceans deep,
In nature's arms, secrets we keep.

(Chorus)
Oh, Earth, you're a wonder, a sight to behold,
Your story, through ages, has been told.
From your blue skies to your green land,
You're a masterpiece, so grand.

(Verse 2)
Forests dense with life abound,
In every corner, beauty is found.
Rivers flowing with graceful might,
Under the moon's gentle light.

(Chorus)
Oh, Earth, with your seasons of change,
```

Figure 2-18. *Copilot can even write beautiful poems for you*

Copilot generates the poem in detail, which you can directly use for your projects. As you can see, Microsoft Copilot can generate any content based on the provided prompt. Let's try something tricky. We asked Copilot to display numbers from 10 to 1, and the response looks as shown in Figure 2-19. You should note that Copilot takes a few seconds to generate the answer. However, you will experience higher speeds if you opt for a Copilot Pro subscription that retails to $20 per month as of July 2024.

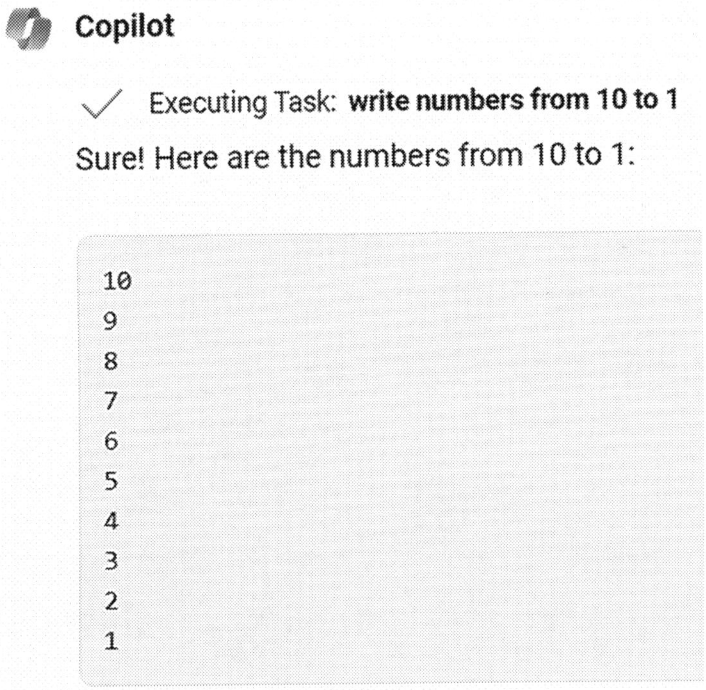

Copilot

✓ Executing Task: **write numbers from 10 to 1**

Sure! Here are the numbers from 10 to 1:

```
10
9
8
7
6
5
4
3
2
1
```

Figure 2-19. Reversing numbers with Copilot

Let's try to gather information related to Medicine with the prompt *Can you explain about the field of Podiatry in less than 250 words?* The query is related to Podiatry, and the output should be within 250 words. In Figure 2-20, you can view the content produced by Microsoft Copilot. You should note that the generated content along with the total word count could vary when you attempt the prompts discussed in this chapter. This is because of the nature of AI.

Figure 2-20. *Copilot produces content based on the prompt*

Copilot provides a concise response within 250 words as specified in the prompt with relevant sources. The interesting point is that Copilot has fetched the results from the website of a hospital near my locality.

In this way, you can request Microsoft Copilot to generate answers based on conditions like the number of words, characters, and much more. You should make sure to double-check the generated content via plagiarism tools if you plan to use the content on your blog.

Let's now ask Copilot to compare two smartphones with the help of Copilot

Prompt: *Write a comparison article on iPhone and Android smartphones in 250 words.*

Conversation Style: *Balanced*

We asked Copilot to produce a general comparison article in 250 words, but the AI chatbot generated a 300-word article, which is good for SEO purposes. The output looks as shown in Figure 2-21.

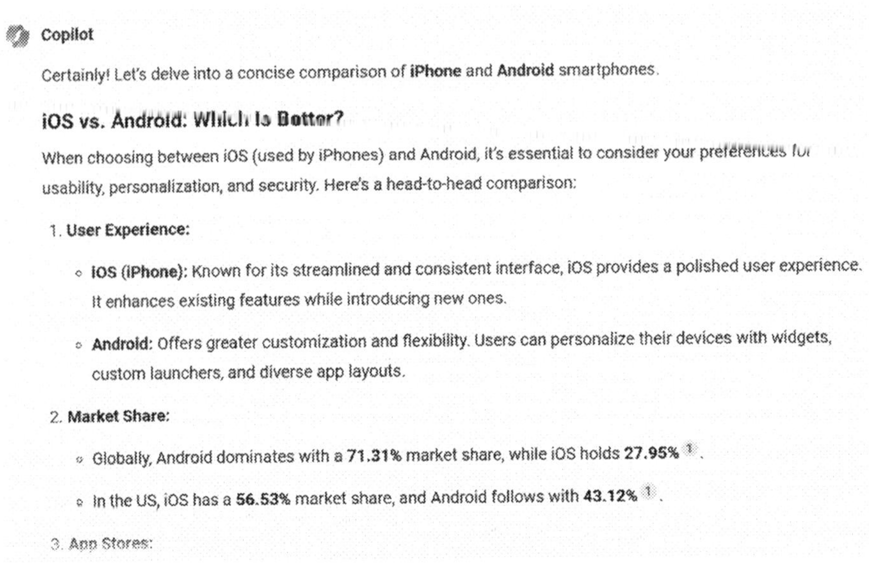

Copilot

Certainly! Let's delve into a concise comparison of **iPhone** and **Android** smartphones.

iOS vs. Android: Which Is Better?

When choosing between iOS (used by iPhones) and Android, it's essential to consider your preferences for usability, personalization, and security. Here's a head-to-head comparison:

1. **User Experience:**

   - **iOS (iPhone):** Known for its streamlined and consistent interface, iOS provides a polished user experience. It enhances existing features while introducing new ones.

   - **Android:** Offers greater customization and flexibility. Users can personalize their devices with widgets, custom launchers, and diverse app layouts.

2. **Market Share:**

   - Globally, Android dominates with a **71.31%** market share, while iOS holds **27.95%** [1].

   - In the US, iOS has a **56.53%** market share, and Android follows with **43.12%** [1].

3. **App Stores:**

Figure 2-21. Copilot capable of delivering detailed content

Copilot generates detailed content in bulleted format. You can easily read the content and publish it on your blog with the required screenshots. As you can see, Copilot is capable of performing all the required tasks as per the relevant prompt. We have observed 99% accuracy in all the outputs. You can make use of Copilot for educational purposes and for publishing content on your blog. Microsoft Copilot is capable of generating even long form articles, which is best suited for SEO.

Working with SEO Using Copilot

Search Engine Optimization (SEO) plays a pivotal role in ranking your content on search engines like Bing and Google. Copilot can help you with the generation of titles, descriptions, and relevant tags. You just need to copy them while composing the article. If you publish via WordPress, then there are plenty of SEO plugins like Yoast and Rank Math, using which you can easily enhance the quality of the content.

Let's try to generate a title, description, and keywords for the preceding smartphone comparison article. You should note that Copilot can produce results even though there is a spelling error on the prompt. The list of titles appears inside the Copilot dashboard as shown in Figure 2-22.

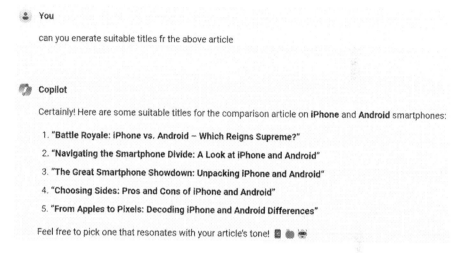

Figure 2-22. *Quickly generate titles via Copilot*

You can pick a suitable title as per your preference. You can also modify the prompt slightly to get better results in case you are not satisfied with the generated titles.

Let's generate an SEO description for the preceding article using Copilot, and the resulting response is displayed in Figure 2-23.

Figure 2-23. *Copilot can generate SEO descriptions*

As you can observe, Copilot accurately generates the SEO description, which you can directly copy to WordPress. Copilot also generates SEO-friendly keywords as featured in Figure 2-24.

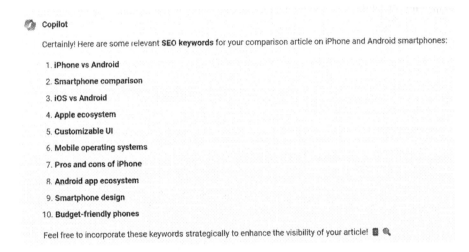

Figure 2-24. *Keywords are important, and Copilot creates them for you*

You can make use of generated keywords to enhance the quality of your content. The keywords can also be added as tags while composing a WordPress blog post. As you can observe, Microsoft Copilot serves as a productive tool not only to generate responses but also to improve the quality of your work.

The Art of Good Prompting

The basic point to note is that you should cultivate excellent prompt writing habits. In addition to the general prompt, you should provide relevant context and situation. Consider the following prompt.

Write an article on best places to visit in San Francisco.

In the preceding example, you are prompting Copilot with a basic question. You can try the following prompt as an alternative. You need not have to worry about spelling mistakes because Copilot will take care of them during the processing of the prompt.

Write an article on best places to visit in a family-friendly location with vegetarian restaurants in San Francisco.

In the preceding prompt, you are asking Copilot to fetch restaurants that are family-friendly with restaurant preferences. Try the preceding two prompts and observe the result yourself. AI chatbots like Microsoft Copilot generate refined responses if you provide a specific context or scenario.

Let's take a look at another scenario with the prompt *Top five laptops.* In this case, you will see the results of all laptops that Copilot fetches for you randomly.

However, you will get better results if you use the prompt *Top five Windows 11 laptops below $400.*

In this case, you are asking Copilot with specific criteria like Windows 11 and pricing. Copilot will deliver a response with a list of laptops as per the specified range. However, the responses vary depending upon various aspects because of the nature of AI. Sometimes, Copilot will fetch a laptop above $400 even if you specify a lower price range. It's all part and parcel of AI technology. Microsoft Copilot generates efficient and accurate responses depending on your prompt.

The art of writing good prompts takes time. You will achieve good results via Copilot only upon experience. If you work with a Windows 11 laptop, try to use Microsoft Copilot to gather information in addition to content, poems, lists, and image generation daily. You can generate accurate images only upon continuous usage. Even though Copilot provides plenty of suggestions for image generation, you should also try to use your prompts. For example, a bird sitting on top of a tree surrounded by flowers with sunset on the backside is an excellent prompt. You should apply your imagination to write good prompts.

Disclaimer   This chapter contains images that are generated via AI onabled Microsoft Copilot. The images are only used for the sake of explanation and educational purposes.

Summary

In this chapter, you have learned about the usage of Copilot using Windows 11 search. This includes a detailed coverage of the Copilot dashboard and the usage of the AI chatbot. You also learned about the working of Microsoft Copilot using various prompts with all conversation styles. You also learned about coding and the generation of SEO-friendly titles, descriptions, and keywords. In the next chapter, you will learn the steps required to work with Copilot in Windows via the Windows 11 Taskbar icon.

CHAPTER 3

Working with Copilot in Windows 11 – Part 2

In Part 1, you have learned the steps to work with Copilot via the Windows 11 search box. In this method, you have to perform multiple tasks such as selecting the Windows 11 search box and then clicking the Copilot icon inside the displayed dialog. Let's work with an easy route in this chapter by selecting the Copilot icon directly from the Windows 11 desktop. Microsoft has integrated Copilot directly on the Windows 11 Taskbar. This is the best and easiest way to work with Copilot since you can work without a web browser. You can explore the AI world by simply selecting the Copilot icon from the Windows 11 Taskbar. Let's get started.

Getting Started

To start working with Copilot in Windows, you should select the *Copilot in Windows (preview)* icon from the Taskbar. You can find the icon either near the search box or on the right side near the *Notifications* icon. The Copilot icon as shown in Figure 3-1 was initially placed near the Windows 11 search box but was relocated to the extreme right side of the desktop for better user experience.

© Anand Narayanaswamy 2024
A. Narayanaswamy, *Microsoft Copilot for Windows 11*, Inside Copilot,
https://doi.org/10.1007/979-8-8688-0583-7_3

Figure 3-1. Hit the Copilot icon

If you select the Copilot icon, you will see a window docked to the right side of the screen as shown in Figure 3-2. You can navigate through the carousel located on the top to work with Copilot-generated prompts. With Windows 11 24H2, Microsoft Copilot will be available as a separate app that can be resized or docked. This means you can open the Copilot app and pin it on the Taskbar. You can open the app as an icon from the Windows 11 desktop.

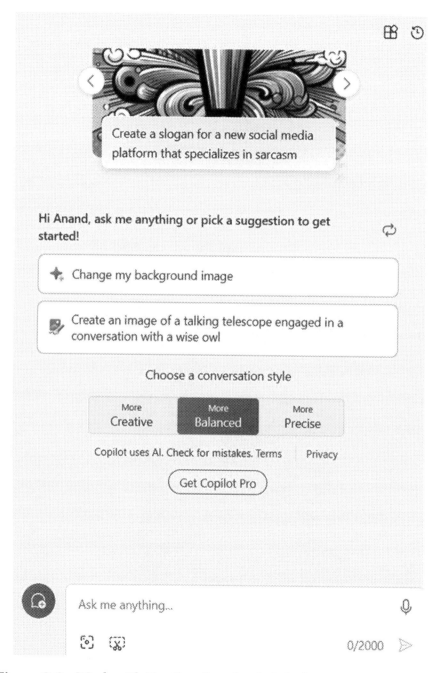

Figure 3-2. Work with Copilot directly via Windows 11

Copilot in Windows (preview) does the same work as discussed in Chapter 2. This includes providing answers to prompts, coding, image creation, and other related tasks. The main benefit of Copilot in Windows is that you can work with the chatbot by selecting the Taskbar icon without navigating to the Windows 11 search.

Note   The Copilot in Windows (preview) icon on the Taskbar animates upon clicking it.

Microsoft has rolled out the integration of Copilot into Windows 11 and is being made available in a phased manner across regions. *Copilot in Windows (preview)* is capable of performing tasks related to Windows, and it varies depending on the region. For example, Figure 3-3 shows the required prompt for changing your Windows 11 desktop to Dark mode from Light mode.

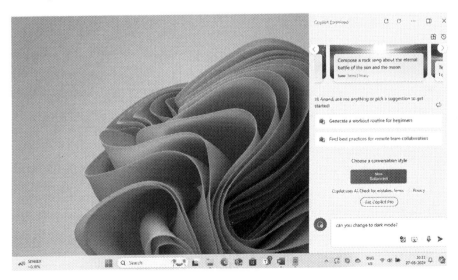

Figure 3-3. Change to Dark mode easily with Copilot

As you can see from Figure 3-3, the Windows 11 desktop is currently in Light mode. You can also view our query on the Copilot dashboard. The Copilot displays a confirmation dialog as shown in Figure 3-4.

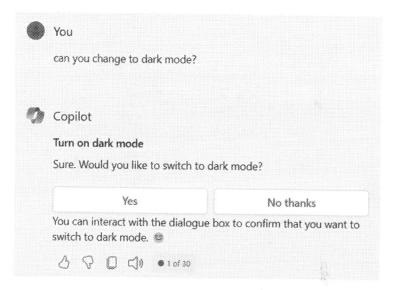

Figure 3-4. *Confirm Copilot directions*

You should click the *Yes* button if you would like to change to Dark mode. If you select the *No thanks* button, then nothing will change. Let's select the *Yes* button and check out the result. Windows 11 immediately changes to Dark mode upon selecting the *Yes* button from the Copilot window as shown in Figure 3-5. You can copy and edit prompt as well as search on Bing if you point mouse cursor over the prompt in Copilot in Windows (preview). The search results will be displayed on the left side of the screen.

Figure 3-5. *Copilot fulfills the changes*

You need not have to navigate to the Settings ➤ Personalization ➤ Colors dashboard to change to Dark mode. Copilot in Windows automatically does all the hard work, thus enhancing your ultimate productivity.

Note   The suggestions provided inside the Copilot in Windows dashboard will change upon each refresh.

Copilot also displays suggested prompts, which enables you to perform actions quickly. Let's now examine another scenario by asking Copilot to open the *Settings* dashboard. You will see a screen as shown in Figure 3-6.

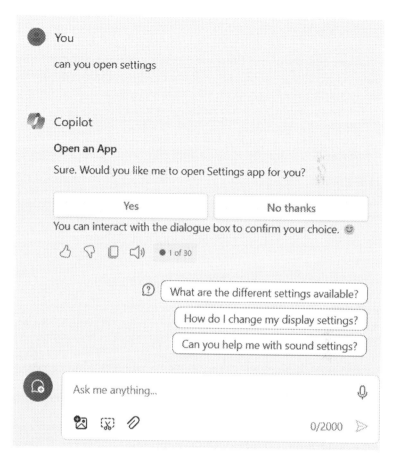

Figure 3-6. *Navigate to Settings via Copilot*

If you click the *Yes* button, Copilot will open the Settings dashboard as shown in Figure 3-7. You can select additional suggested prompts if you would like to explore more about Copilot. This is an easy way to open the Settings dashboard without using the Windows 11 search box or using any keyboard shortcuts. You should note that the Settings dashboard is an important gateway, which provides all the required modules to work with Windows 11 effectively.

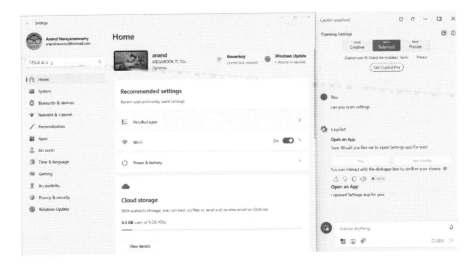

Figure 3-7. *Copilot capable of opening Windows 11 settings*

In Figure 3-7, we have used the Snap Windows functionality using which you can drag and drop windows as per your requirements. You just need to drag the settings dashboard and drag to the top of the display to drop at the desired location.

Performing Windows 11 Tasks with Copilot

The integration of Copilot in Windows 11 enables you to perform several tasks that are related to Windows 11 from within the Copilot dashboard. The ability to change the Windows 11 desktop to Dark theme from Light and vice versa as examined earlier is the main highlight of the Copilot Taskbar icon. You should note that the possibilities are endless, and the tasks mentioned in this section are just a few examples.

Listing Wireless Networks

If you use a prompt such as *List the available wireless networks,* Copilot will immediately display the list of available connections as well as a description as shown in Figure 3-8.

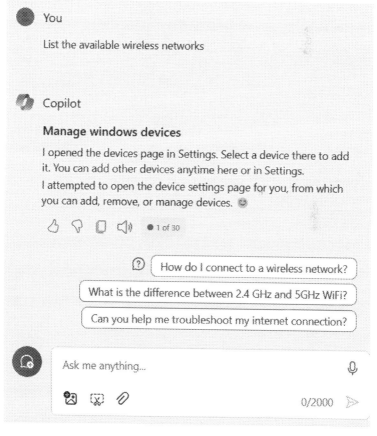

Figure 3-8. *Open networks via Copilot*

If you attempt this prompt on your PC, you will notice that Copilot will not ask for your confirmation while opening the connectivity dashboard. You can easily switch over to other networks without navigating to the Settings dashboard. You will also view additional prompt queries as shown earlier. Copilot in Windows provides detailed explanations if you select these prompts. You can easily learn concepts directly via Copilot without search engine dependency. You should note that the output delivered by Microsoft Copilot could differ if you attempt the above prompt.

Emptying the Recycle Bin

Microsoft Copilot enables you to empty the Recycle Bin. If you provide a prompt like *Can you empty recycle bin*, you will view a screen as shown in Figure 3-9.

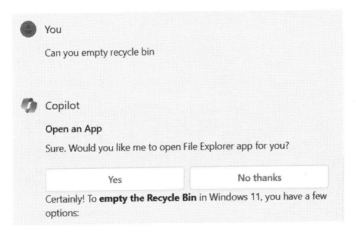

Figure 3-9. *Copilot performs Recycle Bin operations*

Copilot also displays information pertaining to emptying the Recycle Bin, including a related video toward the end of the dashboard.

Displaying Startup Apps

Copilot in Windows can display apps that will load during the booting stage. If you give a *show startup apps* prompt, Copilot will display a screen asking for your confirmation. If you select the *Yes* button, you will see the Task Manager, and a short description like *I opened Task Manager app for you* will appear inside Copilot.

Working with Accessibility Features

Microsoft recently upgraded Copilot in Windows 11 with the ability to help people with disabilities via accessibility functionalities. For example, you can activate a narrator, magnifier, and much more via Copilot. You can modify the text size by giving a prompt like *change text size*, and Copilot will prompt you to open the Settings app. You will also see the steps that should be taken to change text size.

Working with Live Captions via Copilot

You can work with Live Captions via Copilot by providing the prompt *start live captions*. You will see a screen with *Yes* and *No thanks* buttons. If you click the *Yes* option, the settings app will open. You can modify the various Live Captions options via the dashboard. You will not see the exact options related to Live Captions, but you can easily locate them.

Capturing Screenshots

Microsoft Copilot is capable of capturing screenshots. If you provide a prompt like *capture a screenshot*, the Snipping Tool will be activated as shown in Figure 3-10.

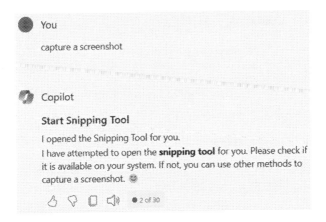

Figure 3-10. *Capture screen via Copilot*

You can then capture the screenshot, and the relevant image will be available inside the Snipping Tool.

Changing Background Image

You can modify the background image of your Windows 11 desktop via Copilot. You just need to simply ask *change background image,* and Copilot will display the Settings dashboard as shown in Figure 3-11.

Figure 3-11. *Copilot helps you to change the background image*

You can easily change the background image by selecting an appropriate option from the Settings dashboard.

Launching Apps

Microsoft Copilot provides the ability to launch apps such as Notepad, Paint, Snipping Tool, and much more. For instance, if you provide the prompt *launch Notepad* and select the *Yes* button, Copilot will open Notepad for you.

Let's check out another example. If you provide a prompt such as *launch calculator*, you will see a screen similar to what you have seen earlier. If you click the *Yes* button, the Calculator app will be opened as displayed in Figure 3-12.

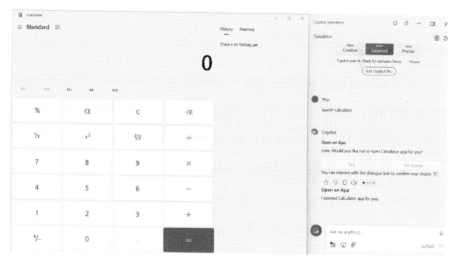

Figure 3-12. *Perform Math via Copilot in Windows*

As you can observe, Copilot automatically opens the Calculator app upon selecting the Yes button.

Activating Focus Session

With the help of Copilot in Windows 11, you can activate a focus session. You just need to provide the required prompt such as *can you start a focus session*. You will see a screenshot as shown in Figure 3-13.

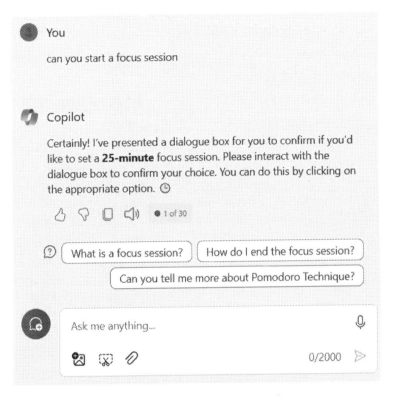

Figure 3-13. *Focus your sessions with Copilot*

As you can see, Copilot displays a message that if you select a dialog box, then the AI chatbot will set a 25-minute focus session. However, we are unable to view any dialog box as mentioned earlier. Microsoft is continuously making improvements to Copilot. It will take time for Copilot to work with ultimate perfection. You can file feedback in case you find any bugs and issues.

Refreshing Copilot

As you continue to work with Microsoft Copilot, the dashboard inside Windows 11 will be filled with prompts and responses. You can reload Copilot in Windows by selecting the *Refresh* icon from the top-right side as shown in Figure 3-14. You should note that the automated suggestions will change upon each refresh.

Figure 3-14. *Start from scratch*

Fetching Copilot Interactions

You can view all your recent interactions with Copilot by selecting the *Recent activity* icon from the top-right side as shown in Figure 3-15.

Figure 3-15. *Recover Copilot History*

Copilot in Windows displays the list of all the recent history upon selecting the *Chats* tab as shown in Figure 3-16. You can scroll down and view the remaining chats.

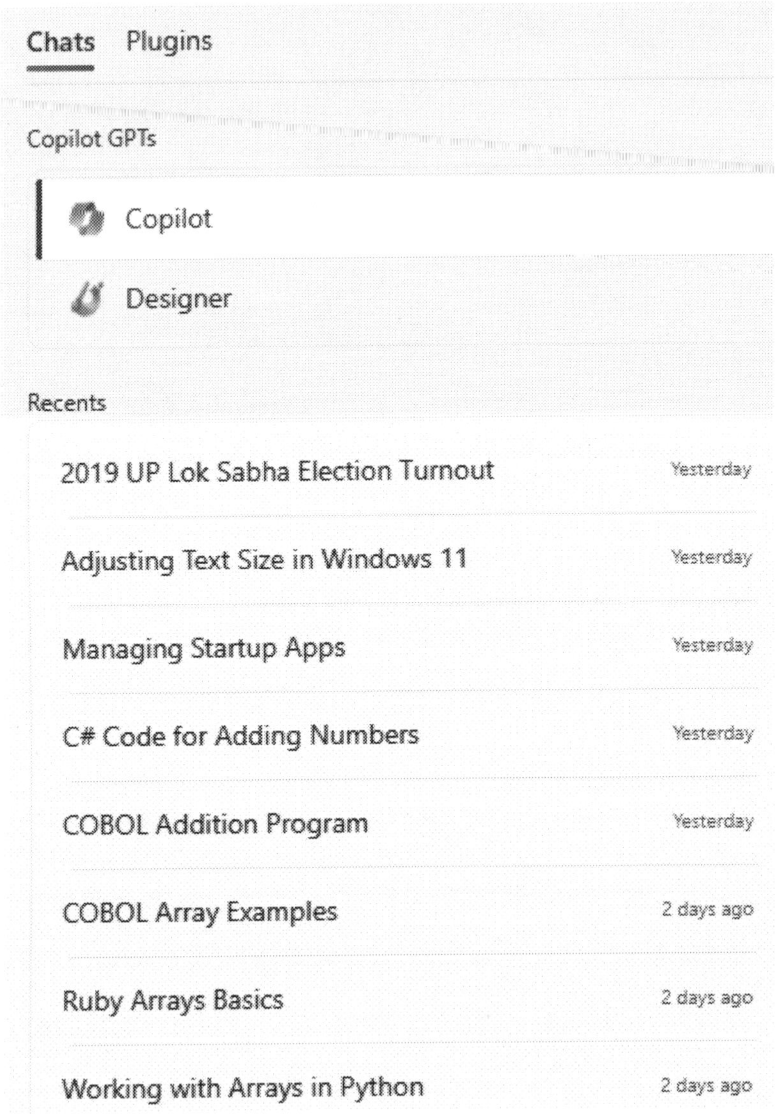

Chats   Plugins

Copilot GPTs

⬤ Copilot

⬡ Designer

Recents

2019 UP Lok Sabha Election Turnout	Yesterday
Adjusting Text Size in Windows 11	Yesterday
Managing Startup Apps	Yesterday
C# Code for Adding Numbers	Yesterday
COBOL Addition Program	Yesterday
COBOL Array Examples	2 days ago
Ruby Arrays Basics	2 days ago
Working with Arrays in Python	2 days ago

Figure 3-16. *View your Copilot History*

If you select the chat titles, Copilot displays the response you viewed previously. You should note that the history will not be saved if you add a work account instead of a personal account.

Note   The active Copilot in Windows (preview) response will open in Microsoft Edge if you select the *Open in Microsoft Edge* icon from the top Toolbar.

You can also select the same prompt from the *Recents* section, and Copilot will provide either the same or a different answer. The response will slightly differ because of the nature of AI technology.

Managing Plugins

You can extend the functioning of Copilot with the help of plugins. You can work with plugins directly from within the Copilot in Windows (preview) Taskbar icon.

Note   You can only activate three plugins for a conversation.

You should select the *Plugins* tab from the *Recent* activity dashboard. Alternatively, you can directly select the Plugins icon as shown in Figure 3-17 from the Copilot in Windows dashboard.

Figure 3-17. *Extend Copilot*

Copilot in Windows 11 displays the list of available plugins as shown in Figure 3-18.

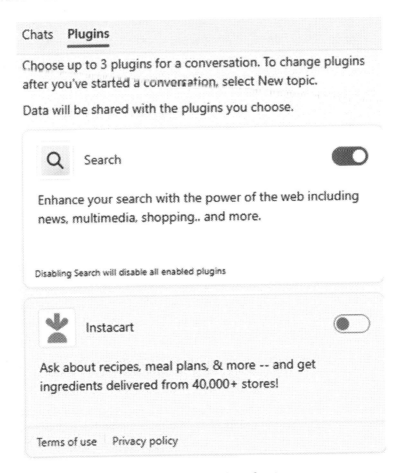

Figure 3-18. Work smarter with Copilot plugins

You just need to activate the plugin and ask queries. For example, you can activate Instacart and ask about your favorite recipe. Copilot in Windows provides support for Search, Instacart, Kayak, Klarna, OpenTable, Shop, and Suno plugins.

Note   The Suno plugin enables you to create royalty-free AI songs, which you can use in your projects.

You should note that the Phone plugin works only via Copilot Web and Copilot Windows apps. You should regularly check the Plugins tab to look for the availability of new plugins. You will learn the usage of Copilot plugins in detail in Chapter 7.

Working with Copilot Notebook

Microsoft Copilot includes a dedicated Notebook module using which you can provide a detailed prompt to interact with the AI chatbot. To work with the tool, you should select the three horizontal dots (see Figure 3-19) and select the *Notebook* option.

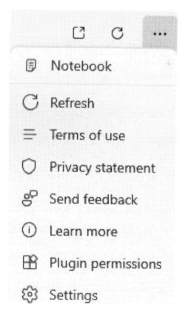

Figure 3-19. *Copilot Notes*

You will see the Notebook dashboard as displayed in Figure 3-20 with options for providing prompts in the form of text, image, or voice.

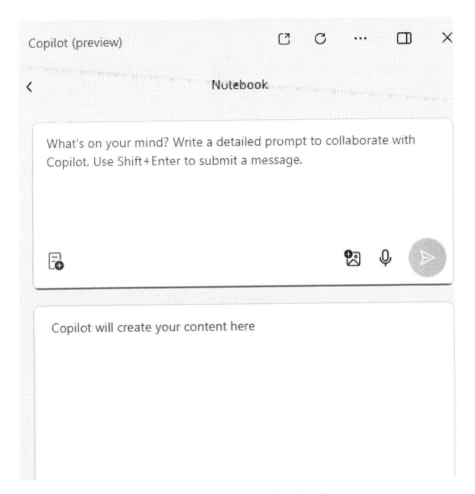

Figure 3-20. *Give longer prompts with Notebook*

The advantage of Notebook is that the tool provides an option for entering a detailed prompt without any distractions. The relevant content will be created directly inside the Notebook dashboard. Let's check out the working of Notebook with a simple prompt as shown in Figure 3-21.

Copilot (preview)
Notebook
Can you write a detailed article on the various Windows editions starting from the first release?

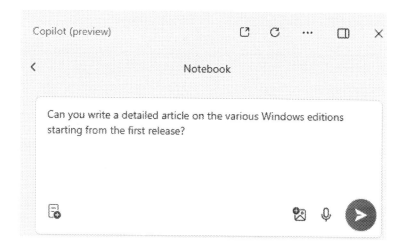

***Figure 3-21.** Sample Notebook prompt*

Copilot Notebook generates the response in bulleted format. The output includes the Windows version number, year, release date, and important features as shown in Figure 3-22.

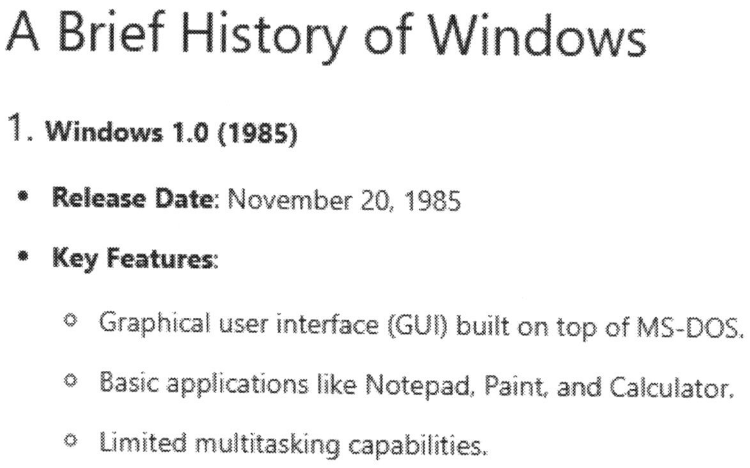

A Brief History of Windows
1. Windows 1.0 (1985)
Release Date: November 20, 1985
Key Features:
Graphical user interface (GUI) built on top of MS-DOS.
Basic applications like Notepad, Paint, and Calculator.
Limited multitasking capabilities.

***Figure 3-22.** Learn Windows 1.0 with Copilot Notebook*

The response also includes information related to Windows 11 as displayed in Figure 3-23.

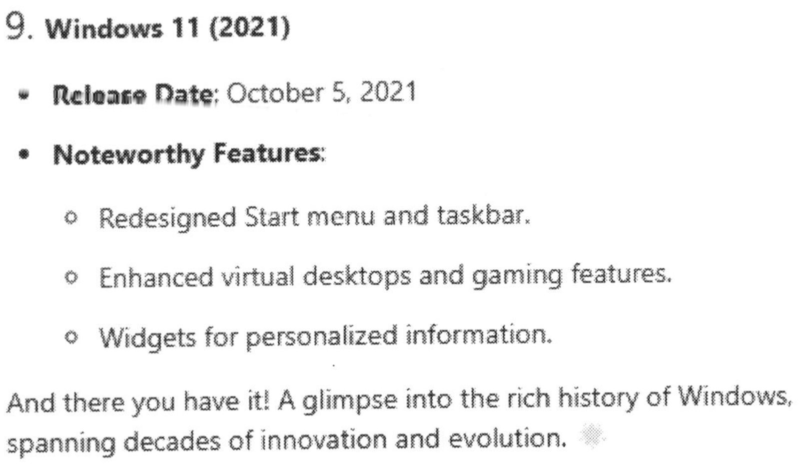

9. **Windows 11 (2021)**

- **Release Date**: October 5, 2021

- **Noteworthy Features**:

  o Redesigned Start menu and taskbar.

  o Enhanced virtual desktops and gaming features.

  o Widgets for personalized information.

And there you have it! A glimpse into the rich history of Windows, spanning decades of innovation and evolution.

Figure 3-23. *Windows 11 in Snapshot*

In this way, you can ask any query using Notebook, and Copilot generates a response with relevant source(s). You can select the *New topic* icon from the prompt textbox as in Figure 3-24 to ask a fresh query without any need to refresh Copilot.

New topic

Figure 3-24. *Launch a new Notebook session*

Note   You can send bug reports by selecting the Send feedback option.

You can also add an image to your prompt by selecting the *Add an image* icon as in Figure 3-25.

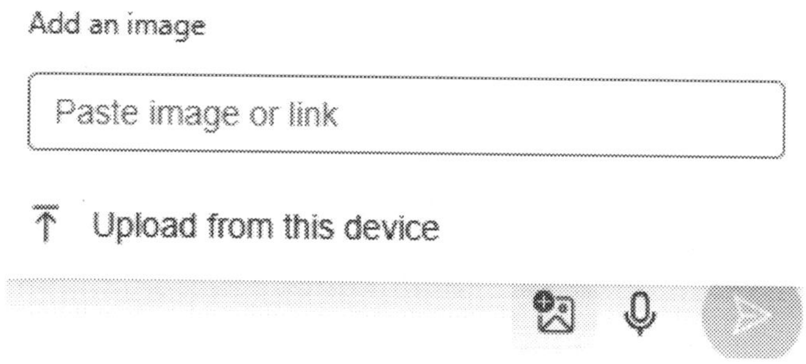

Add an image

Paste image or link

↑   Upload from this device

Figure 3-25. *Upload media and ask Notebook*

You can either provide the image URL or upload the relevant image from your device. Let's upload an image and ask Notebook to identify the items. The resulting output will appear as shown in Figure 3-26.

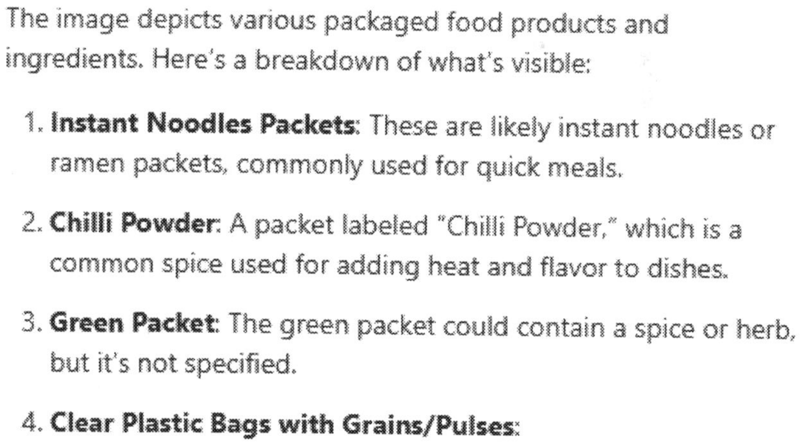

The image depicts various packaged food products and ingredients. Here's a breakdown of what's visible:

1. **Instant Noodles Packets:** These are likely instant noodles or ramen packets, commonly used for quick meals.

2. **Chilli Powder:** A packet labeled "Chilli Powder," which is a common spice used for adding heat and flavor to dishes.

3. **Green Packet:** The green packet could contain a spice or herb, but it's not specified.

4. **Clear Plastic Bags with Grains/Pulses:**

Figure 3-26. *Copilot Notebook fetches Image details nicely*

You should note that Copilot in Windows will not save your interactions with Notebook. You can make use of the content on your blog or social media platforms.

Managing Settings

Copilot in Windows provides one option inside the Settings interface. You can allow Copilot to fetch context suggestions or clues from Microsoft Edge. This option is enabled by default as per Figure 3-27.

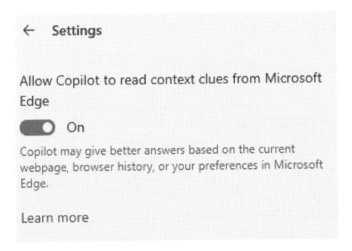

Figure 3-27. *Enable/disable Microsoft Edge permissions*

Microsoft Copilot is capable of delivering better answers based on the current active web page, browser history, or Microsoft Edge preferences.

Managing Visualization

You can change the visual appearance of the way in which Copilot in Windows should be displayed. You can display Copilot in a side-by-side manner by selecting the *Show side by side* option (see Figure 3-28) from the top-right Toolbar.

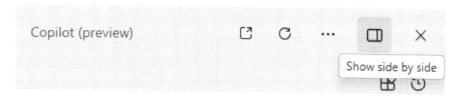

Figure 3-28. Change the way you work with Copilot

If you make use of this option, then all the active windows that you have been working on will be docked to Copilot in Windows as displayed in Figure 3-29.

Note   The width of Copilot in Windows (preview) increases if you select the side-by-side option.

This feature will be useful in cases where you need to simultaneously work with Copilot and the active app. For instance, you can copy the Copilot content directly to either Notepad or Microsoft Word while you work with Copilot.

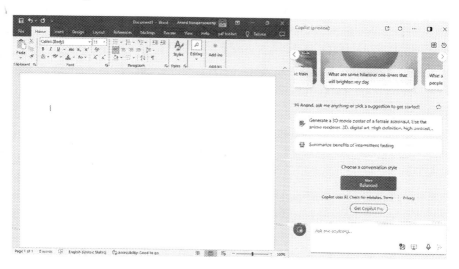

Figure 3-29. Enjoy uninterrupted Copiloting

You can deactivate the side-by-side display behavior by selecting the Show as overlay option as displayed in Figure 3-30.

***Figure 3-30.** Switch to original mode*

As you can observe, Copilot in Windows provides several visual options. You can select an option depending on your requirements. You can also experiment with both options and decide your preferred choice.

Summary

In this chapter, you have learned the usage of Copilot in Windows 11. You will be able to perform several Windows 11 tasks effortlessly, which were normally executed via the Settings dashboard. You also learned about the usage of plugins and Notebook. The chapter also explored the method to view your recent activity with Copilot. Toward the end, you also learned the steps to change the visual options while you work with Copilot. In the next chapter, you will learn the usage of Microsoft Copilot using Microsoft Edge.

CHAPTER 4

Working with Copilot Using Microsoft Edge

Microsoft Edge is a popular web browser included with Windows 11. If you currently work with Windows 11, then you will have access to Microsoft Edge. The Microsoft Edge browser is designed using the Chromium platform. The web browser works fast and is a perfect companion to Windows 11. After the launch of Microsoft Copilot (formerly Bing Chat), Microsoft immediately integrated the AI chatbot into the Edge web browser. The intention was to enable users to work with Copilot from within the web browser without navigating to the search engine interface. Even though the purpose was to help with content creation, Copilot in Edge was integrated with several juicy features. In this chapter, we will explore all the features and the steps to work with Copilot using Microsoft Edge.

Note   You should note that Microsoft updates the user interface and the associated functionalities according to user feedback regularly. Hence, the features and UI could change without any notice.

© Anand Narayanaswamy 2024
A. Narayanaswamy, *Microsoft Copilot for Windows 11*, Inside Copilot,
https://doi.org/10.1007/979-8-8688-0583-7_4

Getting Started

To work with Copilot using Microsoft Edge, you should select the *Microsoft Edge* icon located on the Taskbar as in Figure 4-1.

Figure 4-1. *Discover the power of Copilot with Edge*

You will see the Microsoft Edge web browser loaded with Microsoft Start content from various sources as displayed in Figure 4-2.

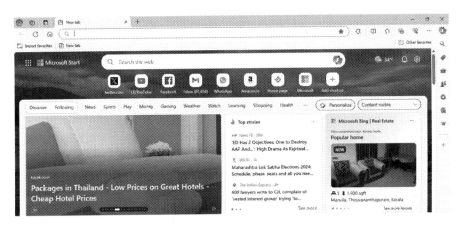

Figure 4-2. *Microsoft Edge dashboard*

You now have two options to work with Copilot in Windows. The first option is to select the *Open Copilot* icon inside the Bing search box after entering the search keyword from the Microsoft Edge home page as shown in Figure 4-3. You can also select specific content from the Microsoft Edge browser and choose *Ask Copilot* option from the pop-up menu. The relevant output will be displayed on the Copilot in Windows (Preview) dashboard.

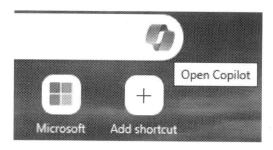

Figure 4-3. *Use the search box on Edge to work with Copilot*

The second option is to point your mouse over the Copilot icon located on the top right-hand side of the Microsoft Edge browser. You need not have to click the icon. In this chapter, you will learn about the features included with this option. You will find several advanced features that you will not find while working with the Copilot dashboard. You will see the Copilot dashboard if you hover over the Copilot icon as shown in Figure 4-4.

Note   You can also make use of the Ctrl+Shift+period keyboard shortcut to open Copilot from within Microsoft Edge. The icon also specifies the key shortcut.

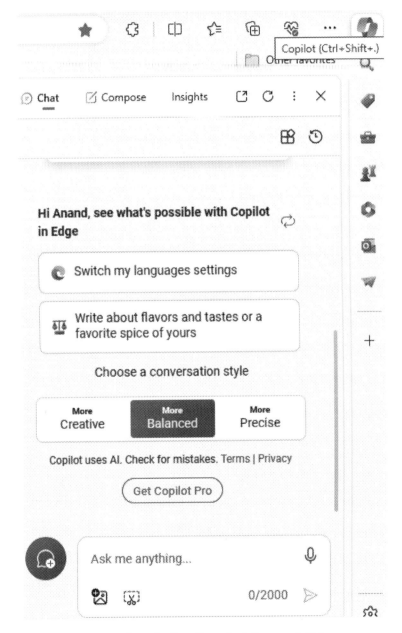

Figure 4-4. *Get started with Copilot via Microsoft Edge*

As you can see, Copilot provides intelligent prompts that you can make use of to work with the chatbot. These prompts will automatically change upon each loading. You can check how Copilot is producing results with the help of these prompts. The default conversation style is Balanced, but you can change to Creative and Precise modes, respectively.

Note   You can work with Copilot by selecting the Copilot in Windows (preview) icon from the Windows 11 Taskbar.

To ask queries, you should provide a prompt up to 2000 characters inside the *Ask me anything* textbox. Let's check out the functioning of Copilot inside Microsoft Edge with the help of a simple prompt as shown in Figure 4-5.

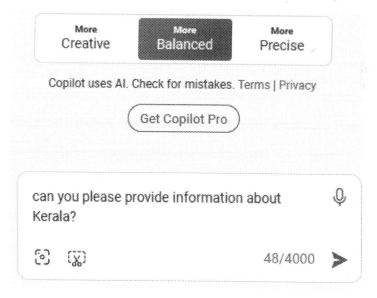

Figure 4-5. Start by giving a prompt

Copilot will provide all the required information relevant to our prompt. The AI chatbot provides information about formation, geography, population, language, nickname, economy, and other facts as displayed in Figure 4-6. You have to scroll down the preview box to view additional information.

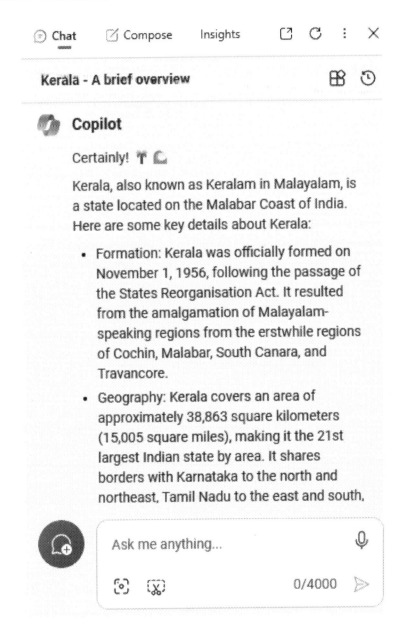

Figure 4-6. *View the Copilot response*

You will be able to know important facts about the state of Kerala within seconds. As you can see, Copilot in Edge delivers responses quickly. Let's now test the functioning of Copilot using a simple prompt in three conversation styles. We are going to try a simple prompt here as shown in Figure 4-7.

Figure 4-7. Intelligent prompting with Copilot

As you can see, Copilot intelligently guesses the prompt and displays the relevant suggestion in grayed format. You can press the *Tab* key to accept the suggestion. In the Balanced mode, Copilot in Windows displays the result as shown in Figure 4-8.

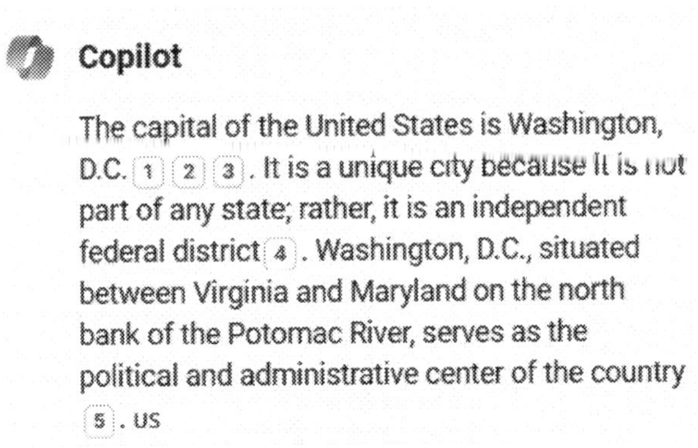

Copilot

The capital of the United States is Washington, D.C. [1] [2] [3]. It is a unique city because it is not part of any state; rather, it is an independent federal district [4]. Washington, D.C., situated between Virginia and Maryland on the north bank of the Potomac River, serves as the political and administrative center of the country [5]. US

Figure 4-8. *Copilot response in Balanced mode*

Let's now switch over to the *Creative* mode with the same prompt. The resulting output is displayed in Figure 4-9.

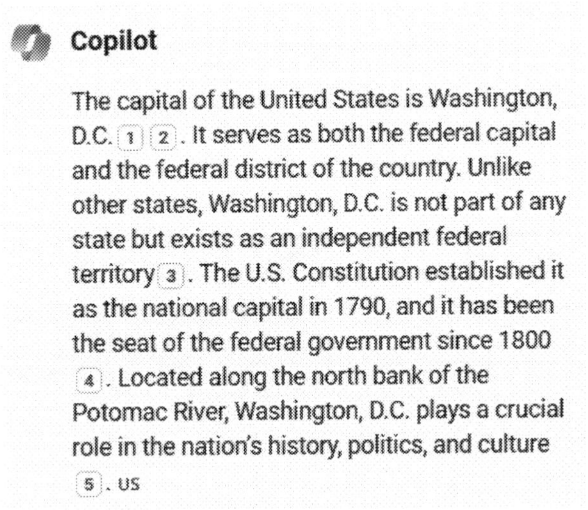

Copilot

The capital of the United States is Washington, D.C. [1] [2]. It serves as both the federal capital and the federal district of the country. Unlike other states, Washington, D.C. is not part of any state but exists as an independent federal territory [3]. The U.S. Constitution established it as the national capital in 1790, and it has been the seat of the federal government since 1800 [4]. Located along the north bank of the Potomac River, Washington, D.C. plays a crucial role in the nation's history, politics, and culture [5]. US

Figure 4-9. *Copilot delivers output creatively*

Let's now examine the output for the same prompt using the *Precise* conversation style. The result is displayed similar as shown in Figure 4-10.

Copilot

The capital of the United States is Washington, D.C. 1 .

Figure 4-10. *Copilot delivers precise information*

As you can observe, Copilot displays the result in one line with the Precise conversation style. You can experiment with the working of Copilot using several prompts with different conversation styles. Microsoft Edge displays a warning message that Copilot makes use of AI, and you should check for mistakes. You can open a PDF file in Microsoft Edge and ask Copilot to summarize the document or locate content from a specific page. Microsoft Copilot is capable of generating highlights from videos. You should open the relevant video on YouTube or Vimeo and select the automated prompt from Copilot in Windows (Preview) or Copilot in Edge. You can also manually provide a prompt like *summarize the video*.

Composing Messages Using Copilot

Microsoft Edge provides an ability to compose new messages for social media, email, and even blog posts. To let Copilot generate content, you should select the *Compose* tab as shown in Figure 4-11.

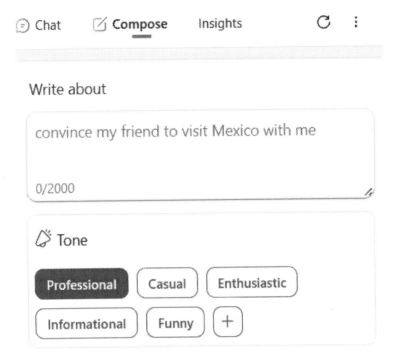

Figure 4-11. *Generate stunning messages with Copilot*

You have to provide the relevant prompt for which you need Copilot to compose content. The next step is to select a tone. The default tone is Professional, but you can select other tones such as Casual, Enthusiastic, Informational, and Funny.

Note   You can also add your own conversation tone by selecting the + icon.

You can select the format of the content such as Paragraph (default), Email, Ideas, and Blog Post. Copilot will attempt to create content based on your selection. The final step is to select the desired length of the content, which defaults to Medium. You can also opt for Short and Long options depending upon your requirements.

Let's try a simple prompt as shown in Figure 4-12 by retaining the default options. You should select *Generate draft* to enable Copilot to create the required content.

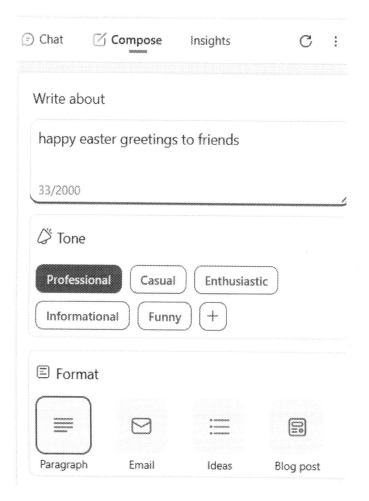

Figure 4-12. *Generate several formats of content with Copilot*

Copilot displays the content as shown in Figure 4-13. You can copy and use the generated message on social media.

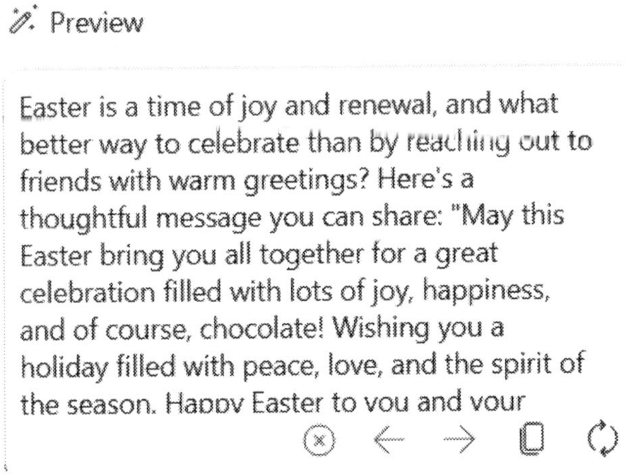

✎ Preview

Easter is a time of joy and renewal, and what
better way to celebrate than by reaching out to
friends with warm greetings? Here's a
thoughtful message you can share: "May this
Easter bring you all together for a great
celebration filled with lots of joy, happiness,
and of course, chocolate! Wishing you a
holiday filled with peace, love, and the spirit of
the season. Happy Easter to you and your

ⓧ ← → ▢ ↻

Figure 4-13. *Copilot generates content inside Edge*

Let's change the tone of the same prompt to *Casual* and check out the
result as displayed in Figure 4-14.

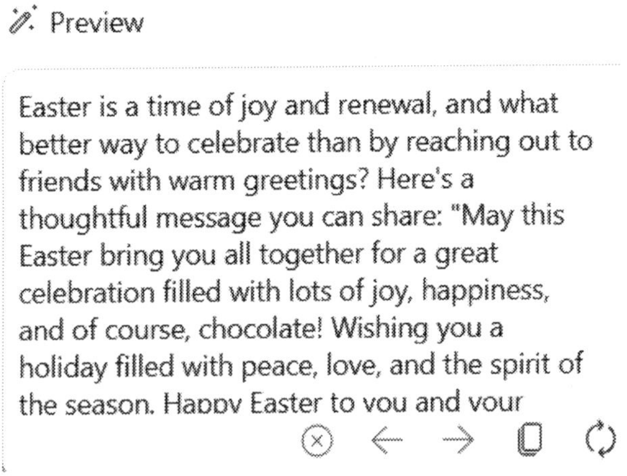

✎ Preview

Easter is a time of joy and renewal, and what
better way to celebrate than by reaching out to
friends with warm greetings? Here's a
thoughtful message you can share: "May this
Easter bring you all together for a great
celebration filled with lots of joy, happiness,
and of course, chocolate! Wishing you a
holiday filled with peace, love, and the spirit of
the season. Happy Easter to you and your

ⓧ ← → ▢ ↻

Figure 4-14. *Copilot's casual content*

If you compare both content, you will notice subtle changes in the
delivery of the message. Let's now change the tone to *Enthusiastic* and
check out the Copilot response in Figure 4-15.

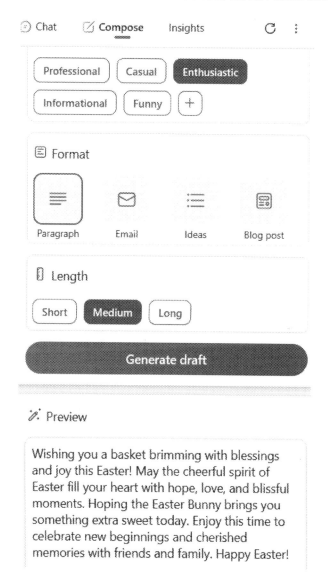

Figure 4-15. *Get responses in Enthusiastic mode*

Even though the first line looks similar, you will notice changes in the remaining content. There are changes to the words, and you can select a tone as per your requirement. The Enthusiastic tone generates shorter content, but it will change upon each attempt. Let's now test-drive with the *Informational* tone as shown in Figure 4-16 using the same prompt.

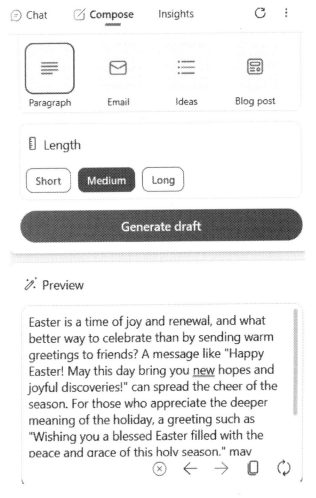

Figure 4-16. *Copilot creates Informative responses*

You can observe that there are plenty of question marks, which are part of the tone structure. The Copilot can also generate content in funny tone. Let's test with another prompt as displayed in Figure 4-17.

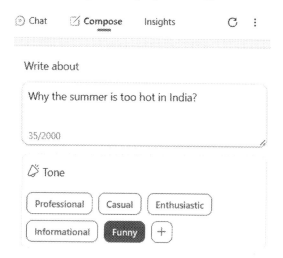

Figure 4-17. *Create funny content via Copilot*

In Figure 4-18, you can view the response delivered by Copilot for the prompt. You can see that the content is different and looks somewhat funny. You can experiment with different prompts and tones to test-drive the functionality of Copilot. You have the required interface to work with AI, and it's up to you to make use of the system optimally. You should use the Copilot module included with the Microsoft Edge responsibly.

✏️ Preview

The summer in India turns into a sizzling cook-off, with temperatures soaring higher than the ambitions of a Bollywood starlet. It's like the sun decides to throw a barbecue and India is the grill! The heatwave is like an uninvited guest that overstays its welcome, turning everything into a sauna session. Reports suggest that this fiery fiesta is due to trapped air that's been sunbathing a bit too long.

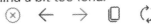

Figure 4-18. *Get funnier with Copilot*

Composing Email Messages

Copilot can also compose email messages based on the relevant prompt. You can select whether you need Short, Medium, and Long length messages. Let's check out the functioning by selecting Email format, Short length, and *April Fool Jokes* as a prompt.

Copilot displays the output as shown in Figure 4-19. You can see that Copilot displays the content in email format, which you can directly copy/paste into your email client.

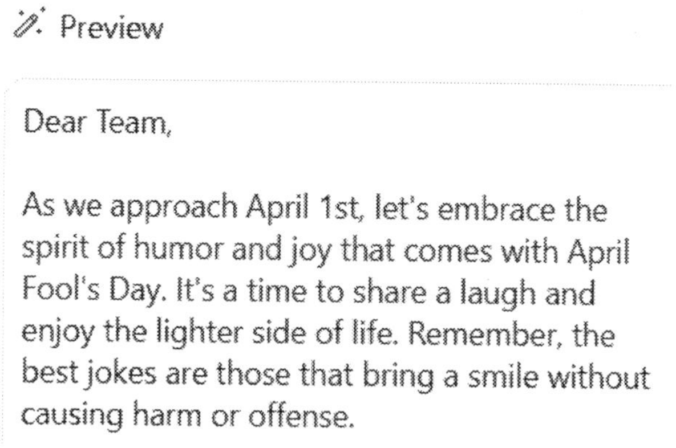

✐ Preview

Dear Team,

As we approach April 1st, let's embrace the spirit of humor and joy that comes with April Fool's Day. It's a time to share a laugh and enjoy the lighter side of life. Remember, the best jokes are those that bring a smile without causing harm or offense.

Figure 4-19. *Create crisp email messages with Copilot*

If you select Medium and Long length formats, then the content will be created accordingly. Copilot can also generate ideas and blog posts. Let's generate some ideas using Copilot regarding computer books. Copilot generates a list of computer books as shown in Figure 4-20. You can then use Amazon to buy the displayed books.

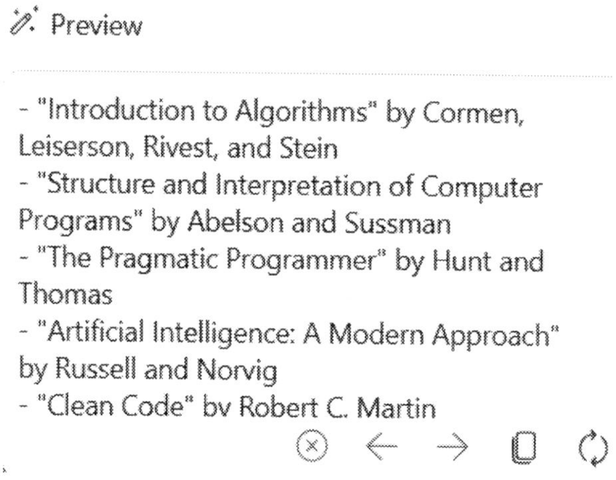

✐ Preview

- "Introduction to Algorithms" by Cormen, Leiserson, Rivest, and Stein
- "Structure and Interpretation of Computer Programs" by Abelson and Sussman
- "The Pragmatic Programmer" by Hunt and Thomas
- "Artificial Intelligence: A Modern Approach" by Russell and Norvig
- "Clean Code" by Robert C. Martin

Figure 4-20. *Generate ideas with Copilot*

You can also ask Copilot to compose a blog post. Let's generate a blog post on *Top 2 Android Smartphones*. Even though we selected Short length format, Copilot generates lengthy content as shown in Figure 4-21. You can scroll down the preview text area to view additional content. You have to test the content for plagiarism using any online tool before publishing on your blog.

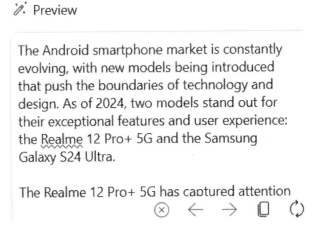

Figure 4-21. *Automate your blog with Copilot*

You can test Medium and Long length formats to view how Copilot generates output. You will be able to know the real usage of the AI-enabled Microsoft Copilot chatbot only if you test the system with various parameters. Make sure you adhere to the guidelines and responsible AI while working with Copilot.

Summary

In this chapter, you have learned the steps required to work with Copilot using Microsoft Edge. You can ask queries and compose content in the form of email and ideas. You can work with Copilot while you browse the Web. You can directly copy the content and publish it on your social media platform or blog. It's so easy that you need not have to navigate elsewhere to work with Copilot because it's built into Microsoft Edge. Microsoft is continuously improving the GPT framework integrated with Copilot, and you have to experiment with the system in several ways. The next chapter examines the usage of Copilot using Bing.

CHAPTER 5

Working with Copilot Using Bing

Microsoft Bing, also called Bing, is a popular search engine since its official launch on June 3, 2009. Bing replaced Microsoft's MSN Search, Windows Live Search, and Live Search. The Bing search engine generates responses in text, images, video, news, and maps in over 40+ languages. The transition from Live Search to Microsoft Bing was announced by the then Microsoft CEO Steve Ballmer on May 28, 2009, during the All Things Digital conference held in San Diego. The search engine was launched with smart search suggestions along with other features.

Microsoft integrated advanced semantic technology from Powerset after its acquisition in 2008. Microsoft also inked a deal with Yahoo for the delivery of search results. Bing was upgraded with the BitFunnel search engine indexing algorithm and other modules of Bing open source. Even though Bing Chat was discussed in Chapter 2, let's distill the facts again shortly. Microsoft refreshed Bing as the new Bing on February 7, 2023, which included a new chatbot named Bing Chat (currently Microsoft Copilot) based on GPT-3 technology. The system was upgraded with GPT-4 technology on March 14, 2023. Microsoft revealed that nearly one million people joined the Limited Preview waitlist within 48 hours. Initially, Bing Chat was only made available to Microsoft Edge and Bing mobile users.

© Anand Narayanaswamy 2024
A. Narayanaswamy, *Microsoft Copilot for Windows 11*, Inside Copilot,
https://doi.org/10.1007/979-8-8688-0583-7_5

Microsoft initially imposed restrictions such as 5 chats per session and 50 chats per day. However, the restrictions were relaxed to 30 chats per session and 300 chats per day on June 2, 2023. Bing hit the 100 million active users landmark in March 2023. Microsoft introduced Bing Image Creator powered by DALL·E 2, which was later on upgraded to DALL·E 3. Microsoft blocked the generation of inappropriate images with sensitive content as part of stringent security measures. Microsoft transformed Bing Chat Limited Preview to Open Preview on May 4, 2023, and the waitlist was eliminated. In July 2023, Bing Chat was made available on non-Edge browsers such as Google Chrome.

Microsoft announced the integration of Bing Chat into Microsoft Copilot on November 15, 2023. You can work with Copilot directly by navigating to the Bing search engine home page. In this chapter, you will learn the steps required to work with Copilot with the help of Microsoft Bing.

Getting Started

To work with Copilot using Bing, you have to navigate to the official Bing portal. You will see a screen as shown in Figure 5-1.

Figure 5-1. *Bing home page*

The next step is to provide a keyword or prompt inside the *Ask me anything* box. Alternatively, you can also search using voice by selecting the microphone icon or search via image by clicking the icon adjacent. Microsoft Bing will display automated suggestions, which you can either select or avoid. The screen looks as in Figure 5-2 after inputting the prompt.

Q Ask me anything...

0/2000

Figure 5-2. *Start your search here*

You should then select the *Copilot* icon located outside the right side of the search box as shown in Figure 5-3.

Figure 5-3. *Copilot icon*

The Copilot dashboard will appear on the screen as displayed in Figure 5-4, and you have to provide the prompt after selecting the relevant conversation style. You can then interact with Copilot by asking queries, coding help, and much more.

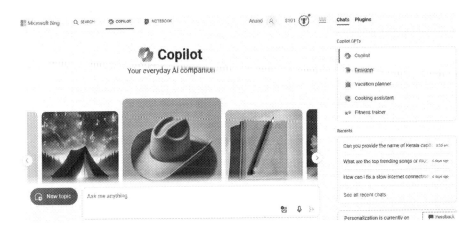

Figure 5-4. *Copilot dashboard via Bing*

You should note that the Copilot dashboard is the same as what you have seen in Chapters 3 and 4. However, the conversation style will not appear sometimes due to the nature of AI technology.

Note   You can work with Microsoft Copilot via Bing using both Microsoft Edge and Google Chrome.

Alternatively, you can also provide a prompt directly in the *Ask me anything* textbox. Let's provide *History of Microsoft* as a prompt inside the search box as shown in Figure 5-5.

Figure 5-5. *Start AI journey directly via the search prompt*

The next step is to select the Copilot logo located on the top-right side. The response will be displayed directly inside the Copilot dashboard as shown in Figure 5-6.

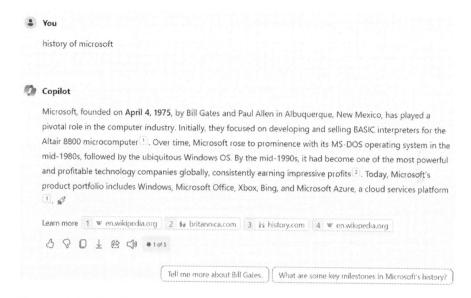

Figure 5-6. *Copilot response after the search prompt*

You can scroll down to view additional content, including automated prompts. For instance, if you select the first prompt as in Figure 5-6, you will see information about Bill Gates. You can also export the generated content in Word, PDF, and text formats by selecting the *Export* icon as shown in Figure 5-7.

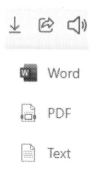

Figure 5-7. *Export and use*

The Microsoft Bing home page also displays predefined prompts. You will see four prompts as displayed in Figure 5-8. You can press the left and right arrows to navigate the prompts.

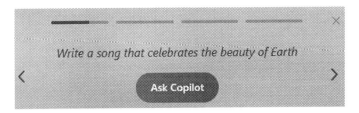

Figure 5-8. *Automated Copilot prompts*

You will see the relevant response inside the Copilot dashboard upon selecting the *Ask Copilot* button. The Bing home page also includes a dedicated Copilot link on the top navigation bar as shown in Figure 5-9. The Copilot dashboard will be displayed upon selecting the link.

Figure 5-9. *Access Copilot from the Bing home page*

It's very easy to work with Copilot via the Microsoft Bing search engine. You can not only work with search as usual but also make use of AI to fetch answers, perform coding related tasks, generating poems, creating listicles, and much more. Microsoft recently announced the integration of a new generative search experience in Bing. Microsoft has combined the power of Large Language Models (LLMs) and Small Language Models (SLMs) with the search results generated by Bing. The results will be displayed in an intuitive and efficient layout. This feature will be rolled out in a phased manner across regions.

Summary

In this chapter, you have learned the usage of Copilot using the Microsoft Bing search engine. The chapter examined the history of Bing, including the evolution of Copilot through Bing. You can easily interact with Microsoft Copilot by giving prompts from the search textbox itself. You also learned the steps to export the Copilot response from the dashboard. In the next chapter, you will learn the application of Copilot in Skype.

CHAPTER 6

Working with Copilot Using Skype

Microsoft has integrated Copilot (formerly Bing Chat) with all its products, including Skype. After the launch of Copilot, the Redmond-based software giant integrated Bing AI Chat into Skype. The Skype messaging platform is used by individuals and companies across the world to interact with each other. The integration of Bing into Skype helped people to ask queries via prompts while they communicate with their colleagues. As of this writing, Microsoft has renamed Bing to Copilot inside Skype, but the change depends on the region. You can follow this chapter even if you have access to Bing AI on Skype. Let's learn the steps required to work with Copilot using Skype.

Getting Started

The first step is to open the *Skype* app from your Windows 11 device. You should then sign in using your Microsoft credentials, which is not required if you had properly configured your PC during the setup process. A running instance of Skype on your PC will appear as a green icon on the right side of the Taskbar. If you open Skype, you will see a verified entry of the Copilot chatbot under the Recent chats panel as shown in Figure 6-1.

© Anand Narayanaswamy 2024
A. Narayanaswamy, *Microsoft Copilot for Windows 11*, Inside Copilot,
https://doi.org/10.1007/979-8-8688-0583-7_6

> **Note**   Alternatively, you can either search for Skype from the Microsoft Store or navigate to `https://apps.microsoft.com/detail/9wzdncrfj364?hl=en-us&gl=IN` manually.

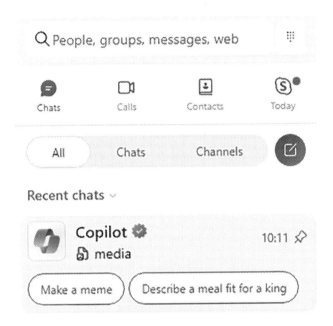

Figure 6-1. *Work with Copilot via Skype*

You can now interact with Copilot as if you are communicating with your friend or colleague. You can provide the prompt inside the *Type a message* textbox, and the results will be displayed inside the chat dashboard. You can also ask queries just like Copilot. Skype also provides automated suggestions as in Figure 6-2. The *Discover Copilot* option enables you to work with trending topics under several categories.

Figure 6-2. *Select a suggested prompt and start*

Fetching Responses

Let's try by asking Copilot to give information about the state of Kerala. Skype will show a progress bar as Copilot in Skype fetches content for you as displayed in Figure 6-3.

Figure 6-3. *Wait until Copilot fetches data*

In Figure 6-4, Copilot in Skype clearly displays all the important information pertaining to Kerala.

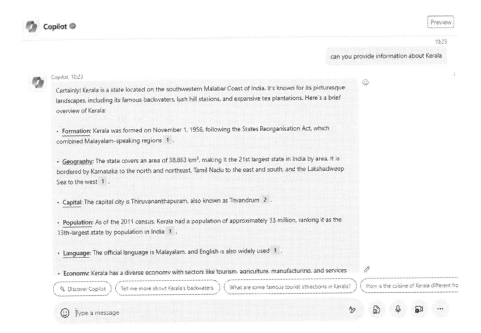

Figure 6-4. *View the Copilot response inside Skype*

You can also click the links included with the content inside Skype, which provides additional information via the Bing search engine. You can then learn more about the topic by selecting the relevant options.

The Copilot chatbot will only display the results. For instance, if you ask the prompt *open calculator*, then the chatbot will display text results with links to several online calculator tools as shown in Figure 6-5.

Copilot, 11:27

I'm unable to open applications or websites directly. However, I can guide you to an online calculator where you can perform your calculations. You can use a website like Online Calculator 1 or Calculator.net 2 for a variety of calculations, from simple arithmetic to more complex equations. Just enter the website address in your browser, and you'll be able to use the calculator right away. If you need help with a specific calculation, feel free to ask!

Learn more:

1. online-calculator.com   2. calculator.net

Discover Copilot   Calculate 25% of 200.   What is the square root of 144?   How do I calculate compound interest?

Type a message

Figure 6-5. *Copilot helps you to work effectively*

You can not only open online calculator tools but also select the automated prompt suggestions. For instance, you can directly select the third prompt and know the square root of 144. However, if you ask the *open calculator* prompt using *Copilot in Windows (preview)*, then you will be able to open the Calculator app directly as shown in Figure 6-6.

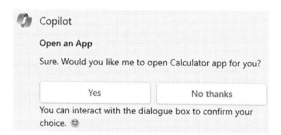

Figure 6-6. *Open the Calculator app using Copilot via Windows 11*

If you press the *Yes* button, then Copilot will open the Calculator app. Microsoft has developed Copilot to work differently as per the relevant app or scenario.

Try Copilot Instantly with Skype

Copilot in Skype also provides a separate module, which enables you to try different topics under diverse categories. This module was previously called Bing examples. To test-drive Copilot, you should select the *Try Copilot* icon as in Figure 6-7, which is located in the top-right corner inside Skype.

Figure 6-7. *Try Copilot from Skype*

You will see plenty of categories as shown in Figure 6-8.

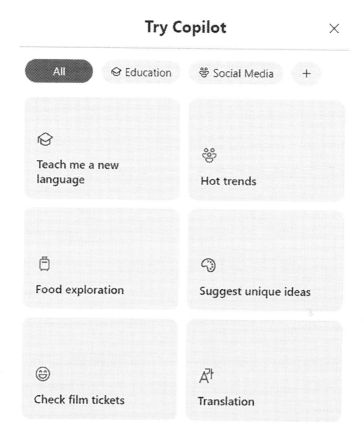

Figure 6-8. Automate Copilot tasks easily

Let's call these options as Copilot examples. You can select a specific category from the tab and select the relevant example that is displayed below. If you select the + icon, you will see additional categories as shown in Figure 6-9.

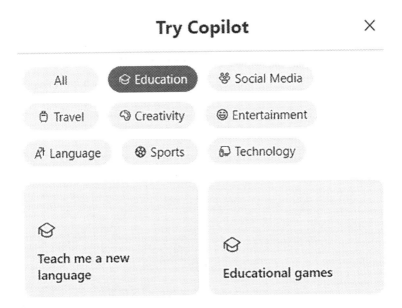

Figure 6-9. *Expand the categories for additional knowledge*

Let's check out the working of Copilot examples by selecting the option *Teach me a new language*. The Copilot chatbot will display the relevant prompt inside Skype as shown in Figure 6-10.

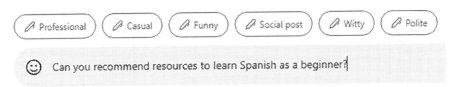

Figure 6-10. *Automated prompt upon selection*

The Copilot chatbot in Skype displays the resulting output as in Figure 6-11 with information related to online courses and videos, websites, apps, podcasts, and other resources for learning Spanish. Copilot also provides automated suggestions related to the Spanish language, which you can select for additional learning.

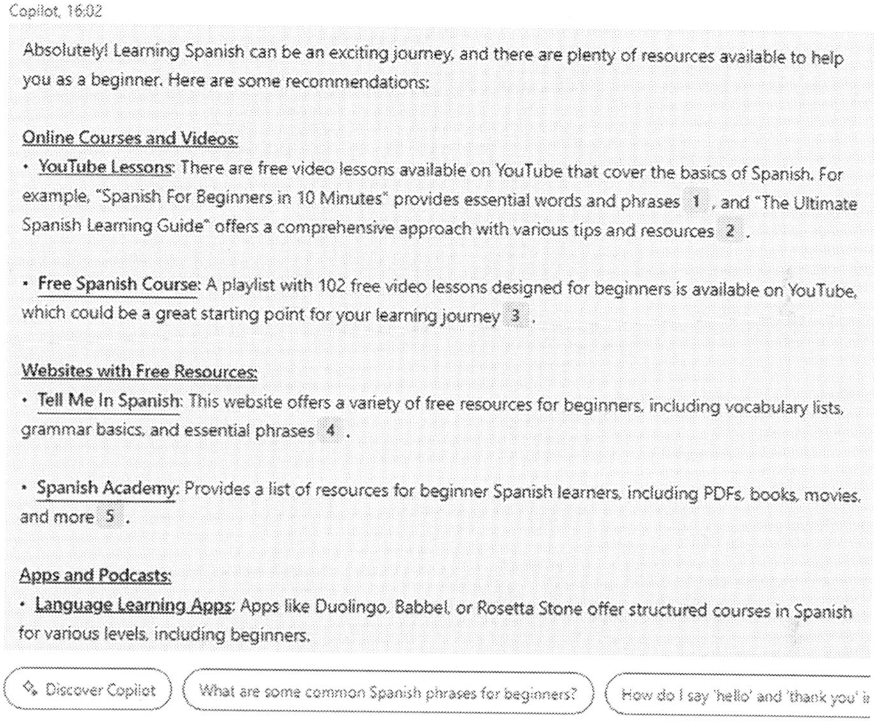

Copilot, 16:02

Absolutely! Learning Spanish can be an exciting journey, and there are plenty of resources available to help you as a beginner. Here are some recommendations:

Online Courses and Videos:
• YouTube Lessons: There are free video lessons available on YouTube that cover the basics of Spanish. For example, "Spanish For Beginners in 10 Minutes" provides essential words and phrases 1 , and "The Ultimate Spanish Learning Guide" offers a comprehensive approach with various tips and resources 2 .

• Free Spanish Course: A playlist with 102 free video lessons designed for beginners is available on YouTube, which could be a great starting point for your learning journey 3 .

Websites with Free Resources:
• Tell Me In Spanish: This website offers a variety of free resources for beginners, including vocabulary lists, grammar basics, and essential phrases 4 .

• Spanish Academy: Provides a list of resources for beginner Spanish learners, including PDFs, books, movies, and more 5 .

Apps and Podcasts:
• Language Learning Apps: Apps like Duolingo, Babbel, or Rosetta Stone offer structured courses in Spanish for various levels, including beginners.

✦ Discover Copilot   What are some common Spanish phrases for beginners?   How do I say 'hello' and 'thank you' in

Figure 6-11. *Fetch information easily inside Skype*

Let's test another Bing example by selecting the *Technology* category and *Tech support* example as in Figure 6-12.

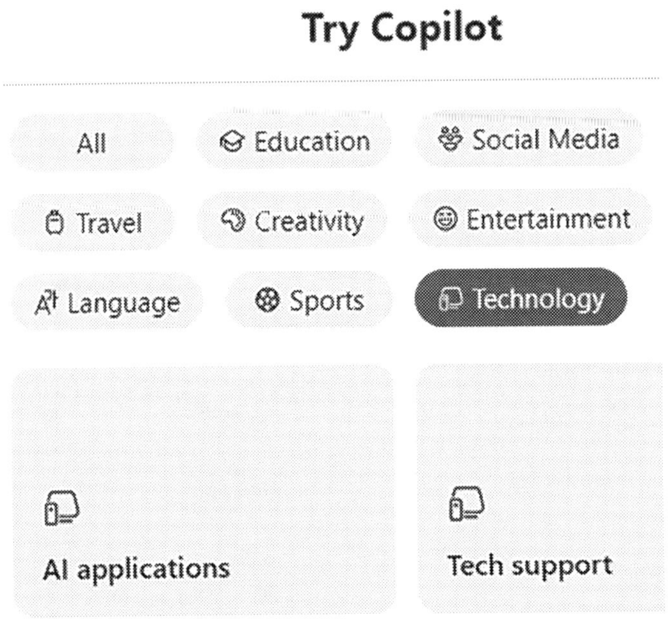

Try Copilot
All
Education
Social Media
Travel
Creativity
Entertainment
Language
Sports
Technology
AI applications
Tech support

Figure 6-12. *Get free tech support via Copilot*

Change Content Tone Easily

Copilot automatically displays the prompt as in Figure 6-13. As you can observe, Bing displays several tones such as Professional, Casual, Funny, Social post, Witty, and Polite.

Professional
Casual
Funny
Social post
Witty
Polite
How can I fix a slow internet connection on my computer?

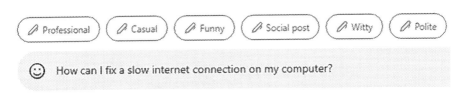

Figure 6-13. *Select a tone and generate a response*

Let's select the Social Post tone and observe the result as in Figure 6-14. You can directly copy the generated content by selecting the *Copy message* icon located on the right side. Copilot also generates AI images from within Skype. You can download them to your PC and use them on your social media and blog post. It's very easy to create not only content but also images driven by DALL·E 3 technology.

Figure 6-14. *Create social media content quickly*

If you select the *Update* button, a new prompt will be generated by Copilot in Skype. Let's now change to the *Entertainment* category and select the *Music* example. Copilot displays a prompt as shown in Figure 6-15.

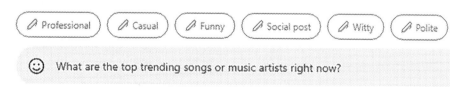

Figure 6-15. *Fetch answers to your music queries*

Let's select the *Funny* tone, and the prompt will change as shown in Figure 6-16.

111

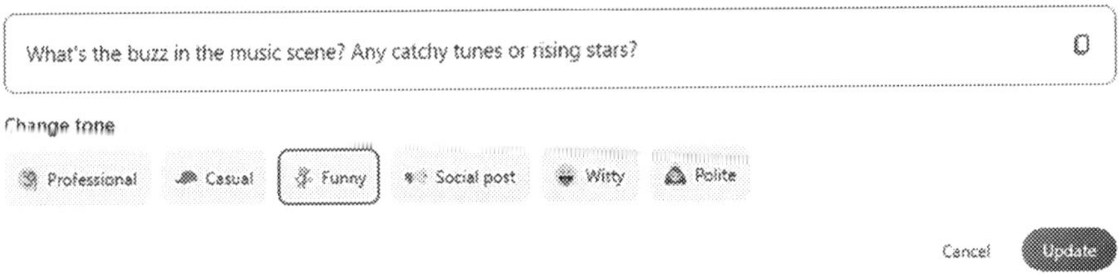

What's the buzz in the music scene? Any catchy tunes or rising stars?
Change tone
Professional
Casual
Funny
Social post
Witty
Polite
Cancel
Update

Figure 6-16. *Automatically change prompts via AI*

If you select the *Update* button, the revised prompt will appear inside the textbox. You can ask Copilot in Skype to generate answers based on the Funny conversation tone.

Using Copilot in Group Chats

You can either chat directly with Copilot in Skype or interact with your friends via group chat. If you are not part of any group, you can test the functionality by selecting *New Chat* icon as shown in Figure 6-17.

All
Chats
Channels
Recent chats
New Chat
Copilot
13:40
I'm designed for one-on-one...
Write a postcard from 2110

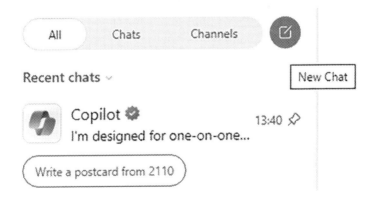

Figure 6-17. *Starting to create a group chat*

The next step is to select *New Group Chat* option from the displayed pop-up menu as shown in Figure 6-18.

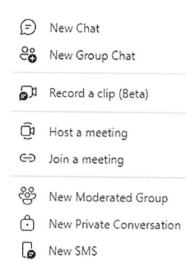

Figure 6-18. *Creating a group chat*

You have to add a name for your group and select the member(s) from the displayed list. You also need to add Copilot as a member of your group, which appears while adding members as shown in Figure 6-19.

Figure 6-19. *Adding a Copilot*

The newly created group appears on the screen, and the concerned member will be notified. Copilot is now part of a group on Skype. You can interact with Copilot by using the *@Copilot* mention from within a group chat. Let's test the functionality by asking Copilot to provide more information about Apress, and the resulting response is shown in Figure 6-20.

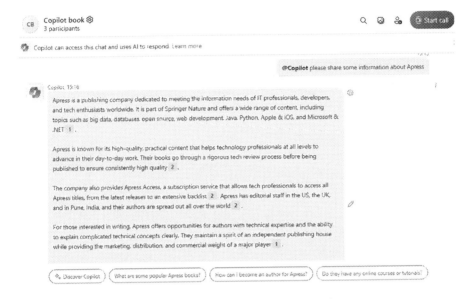

Figure 6-20. *Copilot in action via Skype group chat*

Copilot in Skype also provides the ability to summarize chats. In Figure 6-21, you can view the response generated by Copilot for the prompt *Can you summarize the chat in the last 1 hour?*

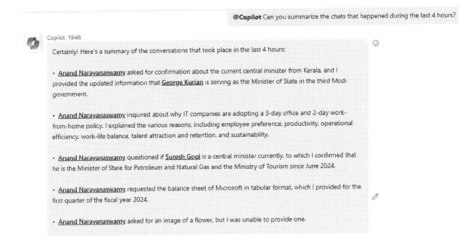

Figure 6-21. *Copilot summarizes Skype group chats*

You can also ask Copilot to summarize chats in the last 24 hours or 2 days like that. Copilot displays the point-wise summary. You should note that Copilot is an effective productivity tool when combined with group chats. However, audio and video interactions are not supported in Skype. Even though Copilot generates responses based on reliable sources, the system could make errors. This is the nature of AI. However, you can double-check the facts and information provided by Copilot.

Summary

In this chapter, you have learned the workings of Copilot in Skype. You can ask queries just like you do with Copilot. Moreover, intelligent prompt suggestions help you to fetch answers quickly. The bundled Copilot examples enable you to learn more about various prompts that are divided into several categories. You should note that Microsoft recently replaced the original Bing AI in Skype with Copilot. If you view Bing inside Skype, then the steps discussed in this chapter are the same. Skype displays Bing progress text instead of Copilot, and the content rendering will be the same. Moreover, the Try Copilot examples module will be named as Bing examples. The conversation tones will also be the same as Copilot in Skype. Microsoft renamed all instances of Bing as Copilot for the sake of uniformity. In the next chapter, you will learn the usage of Copilot Web.

CHAPTER 7

Working with Copilot Web

In the previous chapters, you have learned the usage of Copilot using Windows 11, Microsoft Edge, Bing search engine, and Skype. Microsoft has provided several ways to access Copilot. Even though you can easily access Copilot directly by selecting the icon from the Windows 11 Taskbar, you can also directly navigate to the Copilot web interface to work with the AI chatbot. You have already seen the Copilot web user interface in the previous chapters. In this chapter, you will learn all the modules such as GPTs and plugins that are included with the Microsoft Copilot web dashboard. Let's get started.

Getting Started

To work with Copilot Web, you should navigate to `https://copilot.microsoft.com`. You will see a dashboard as shown in Figure 7-1.

© Anand Narayanaswamy 2024
A. Narayanaswamy, *Microsoft Copilot for Windows 11*, Inside Copilot,
https://doi.org/10.1007/979-8-8688-0583-7_7

Figure 7-1. *Work with the Copilot dashboard*

You have to provide the relevant prompt and select the suitable conversation style (see Figure 7-2) by scrolling down to the Copilot dashboard. Microsoft is currently experimenting a new Copilot user interface without conversation styles. However, the styles appear randomly for free users, but they appear permanently for Copilot Pro users. Microsoft hasn't revealed that the three styles are reserved only for Copilot Pro users. Even if you are not a Copilot Pro subscriber, the conversation styles can be enabled by navigating to *Settings* and changing the *Country/Region* to *United States - English*. You can also change the appearance of the Copilot web interface to Dark. You will see the relevant options by selecting the three horizontal lines (hamburger menu) adjacent to the Profile icon.

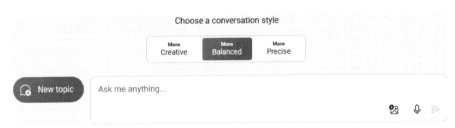

Figure 7-2. *Get answers to all your queries*

The default style is Balanced, but you can switch over to Creative and Precise if required. Refer to Chapter 2 to learn about the various use cases of these three conversation styles in detail.

Note   The Copilot dashboard displays several automated prompts based on several topics. The Copilot chatbot displays the response upon selecting the relevant prompt.

Working with Copilot GPTs

Microsoft has released Copilot GPTs which can be accessed from the Copilot Web dashboard. You can access Copilot GPTs from the right side of the dashboard as displayed in Figure 7-3. You should note that Microsoft has announced the retirement of GPT Builder in July 2024 for Consumer Copilot. This means all GPTs created by Microsoft and that of the end user along with the associated data have been deleted. However, the GPT Builder will be available for Commercial and Enterprise users.

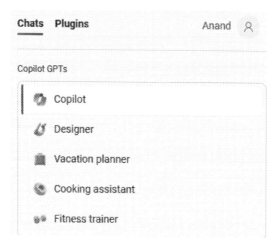

Figure 7-3. *Create and plan with automated GPTs*

119

The default option is Copilot, and it's the option you are currently working on. You can fetch answers to prompts as well as write long articles, lists, poems, and much more.

Generating Images with Copilot

Microsoft Copilot enables you to generate stunning images for various requirements. You can easily create AI images directly from the Copilot dashboard via Designer GPT. Moreover, you can also generate images via Copilot in Windows (preview), Copilot Web, Skype and Copilot Windows app. Let's try to create an AI image.

Prompt: *Create images of vegetable pizza along with hot brewing coffee on the table.*

You should select Designer GPT and provide the preceding prompt. Copilot Designer takes a few seconds to generate images since it involves enormous processing. The generated image will be displayed on the dashboard.

Note   You can try the preceding prompt using Microsoft Copilot and observe the output. The AI system is developed in such a way as to generate different responses upon each attempt.

You can export and share the generated image by selecting the relevant icons as shown in Figure 7-4. You can share via email, Facebook, X (formerly Twitter), Pinterest, LinkedIn, Reddit, and OneNote. You can also copy the link and manually share via social media platforms and blogs.

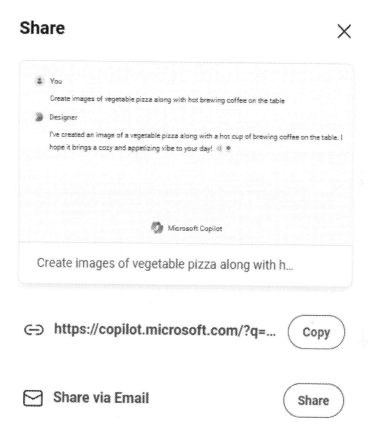

Figure 7-4. Reveal the images to others instantly

You can also download the generated AI images. For this purpose, you have to select an image. The enlarged version will appear inside the dashboard. The generated image slightly animates upon selection.

You have to select the three horizontal dots located on the top-right side of the enlarged image. The next step is to select the *Download* option as shown in Figure 7-5.

Figure 7-5. *Share the image*

The relevant image will be downloaded to your system upon selecting the *Download* option, and a confirmation message will be displayed.

Note   The AI image generation tools are trained on massive datasets of images including other creative works.

If you select the *Edit in designer* option, Copilot will prompt you to open the Designer editor in a new tab. You will see the Designer editor upon selecting the option displayed in Figure 7-6. You can add filters and effects with the help of various options via the dashboard. You can observe how the generated image based on the prompt appears inside the editor.

Figure 7-6. *Microsoft Designer in action with Copilot-generated image*

Note   You should note that the images generated by Microsoft Copilot differ when you attempt the same prompt. AI chatbots and systems are developed to generate different images upon each attempt.

Planning Vacations

The *Vacation planner* GPT provides a dedicated dashboard for planning vacations. You can discover new destinations, create itineraries, and also enable users to book travels. The dashboard looks as shown in Figure 7-7.

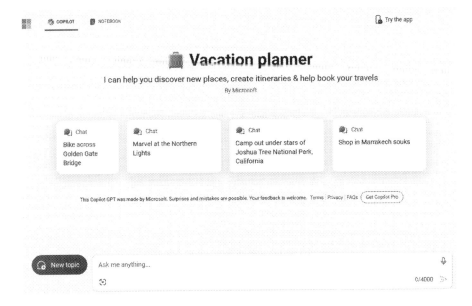

Figure 7-7. *Check Copilot and plan vacations*

The Vacation planner GPT provides a few predefined prompts using which you can test the working. Let's test-drive the working of the GPT by providing a prompt.

Prompt: *Create a detailed vacation planner with places to visit in Thiruvananthapuram.*

The Copilot Vacation planner GPT renders a detailed output (Figure 7-8) spanning over four days along with a map and nearest spots to explore. You can also add unique data to your prompt like veg hotel, type of food, and much more to refine the Copilot output.

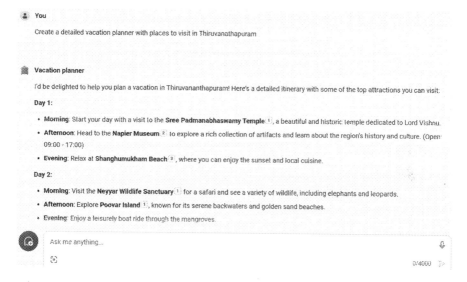

Figure 7-8. *Explore places with Copilot*

In this way, you can play with the Vacation planner GPT. Copilot is so powerful that it renders accurate information. Moreover, the Vacation Planner GPT also provides prompt suggestions as shown in Figure 7-9.

Figure 7-9. *Make use of Copilot-generated prompts*

Cooking with Copilot

Are you wondering whether it's possible to cook with Copilot? Even though you can't cook food via Copilot, the AI chatbot can guide you to cook food. You can ask Copilot to locate recipes, create meal plans, and fetch cooking tips and tricks using Cooking assistant GPT. The dashboard looks like as displayed in Figure 7-10.

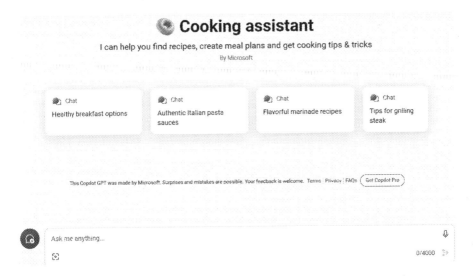

Figure 7-10. *Cooking made simple with Copilot*

The dashboard displays predefined prompts, which you can make use of to test-drive Copilot. You can also provide your own prompt as shown in Figure 7-11.

Figure 7-11. *Ask Copilot about any recipe*

The prompt requests Copilot to create a recipe for preparing South Indian dish Sambar. The grayed portion is suggested by Copilot and will be added upon pressing the Tab key. The displayed word is part of the Tamil language, and it translates to rice. Copilot displays the response with the list of ingredients and detailed instructions as shown in Figure 7-12.

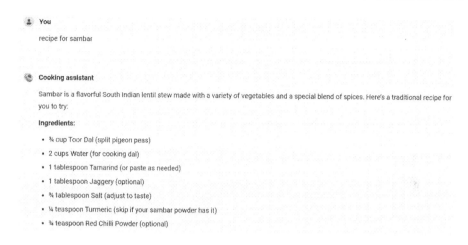

Figure 7-12. *View the recipe generated by Copilot*

Do you want to copy, edit prompt and search on Bing from the Copilot dashboard? You just need to point mouse cursor over the prompt. The search results will be displayed in a new window. Toward the end, Copilot displays the recipes that can be accessed from various third-party sources with thumbnails. Moreover, Copilot also displays the suggested prompts, which you can use to learn additional information about the dish. You can use Cooking assistant GPT to create information related to cooking. This exclusive GPT will be very useful for homemakers since they can easily locate the recipe they are looking for without navigating the complex paginated search results.

Monitor Your Health with Copilot

You can manage your health with Microsoft Copilot with the help of *Fitness trainer* GPT as shown in Figure 7-13. Copilot enables you to design exercise programs in addition to delivering informative content about nutrition, health, and wellness.

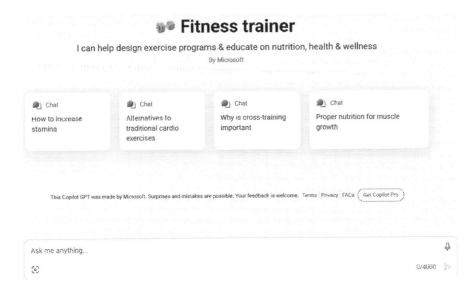

Figure 7-13. *Live healthy with Copilot*

As usual, the Fitness trainer displayed prompts that you can use to test-drive the GPT module. Let's test the trainer by using a prompt as displayed in Figure 7-14.

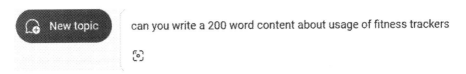

Figure 7-14. *Ask fitness-related queries with Copilot*

Copilot displays a long and crisp article about the usage of fitness trackers as shown in Figure 7-15.

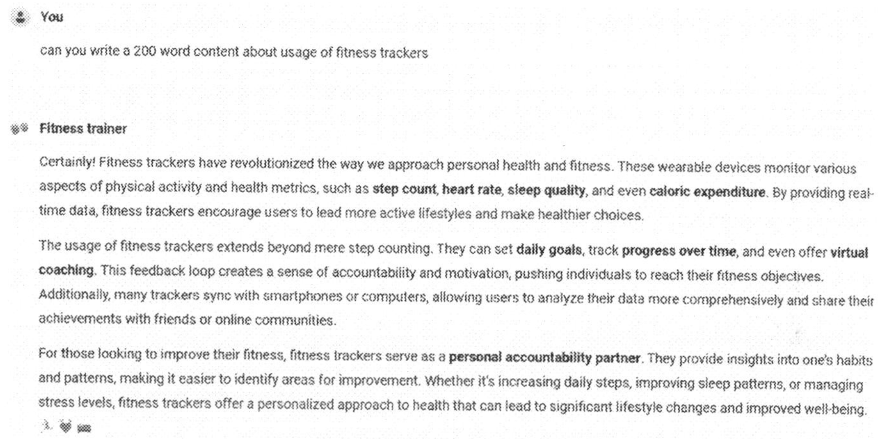

You

can you write a 200 word content about usage of fitness trackers

Fitness trainer

Certainly! Fitness trackers have revolutionized the way we approach personal health and fitness. These wearable devices monitor various aspects of physical activity and health metrics, such as **step count**, **heart rate**, **sleep quality**, and even **caloric expenditure**. By providing real-time data, fitness trackers encourage users to lead more active lifestyles and make healthier choices.

The usage of fitness trackers extends beyond mere step counting. They can set **daily goals**, track **progress over time**, and even offer **virtual coaching**. This feedback loop creates a sense of accountability and motivation, pushing individuals to reach their fitness objectives. Additionally, many trackers sync with smartphones or computers, allowing users to analyze their data more comprehensively and share their achievements with friends or online communities.

For those looking to improve their fitness, fitness trackers serve as a **personal accountability partner**. They provide insights into one's habits and patterns, making it easier to identify areas for improvement. Whether it's increasing daily steps, improving sleep patterns, or managing stress levels, fitness trackers offer a personalized approach to health that can lead to significant lifestyle changes and improved well-being.

Figure 7-15. *Copilot delivers fitness stories*

In this way, you can select the relevant Copilot GPT and ask queries via prompts. These niche-specific GPTs are a great way to fetch information relevant to your topic of interest. You can create custom copilots and customize Copilot for Microsoft 365 using Copilot Studio. You can build copilots via a graphical development environment comprising of sophisticated dialog, knowledge, actions as well as integrated advanced analytics.

Working with Copilot Notebook

In addition to the stand-alone chatbot and dedicated GPTs, Microsoft Copilot also provides a dedicated Notebook module. You can provide a detailed prompt to interact and collaborate with Copilot from the Notebook dashboard in Figure 7-16. Even though you have learned about Notebook in Chapter 2, this section provides a detailed coverage.

Note While Microsoft Copilot accepts up to 4000 characters, Notebook provides support for prompts up to 18,000 characters.

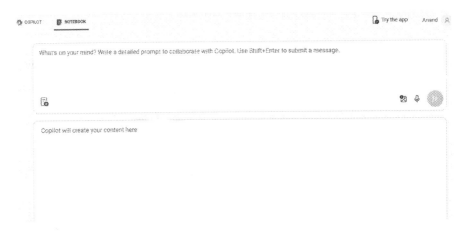

Figure 7-16. *Use Copilot for detailed notes*

You can either select the *Submit* button or make use of the *Shift+Enter* keyboard shortcut after providing the detailed prompt as shown in Figure 7-17.

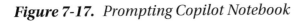

My neighbor's baby reached my house after school. Her house was locked because her mother went to attend coaching classes. However, she has been crying for over 45 minutes. I did all things like giving toys and also switched on TV cartoons. Can you generate a suitable poem, that I can render so that the baby will stop crying?

Figure 7-17. *Prompting Copilot Notebook*

Notebook generates the required poem and displays it on the bottom panel as displayed in Figure 7-18.

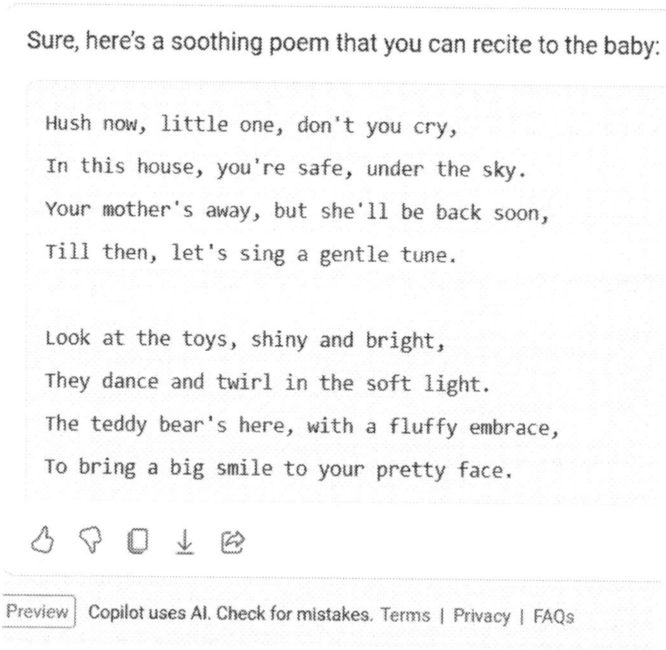

Sure, here's a soothing poem that you can recite to the baby:

```
Hush now, little one, don't you cry,
In this house, you're safe, under the sky.
Your mother's away, but she'll be back soon,
Till then, let's sing a gentle tune.


Look at the toys, shiny and bright,
They dance and twirl in the soft light.
The teddy bear's here, with a fluffy embrace,
To bring a big smile to your pretty face.
```

👍 👎 🗐 ↓ ↪

Preview | Copilot uses AI. Check for mistakes. Terms | Privacy | FAQs

Figure 7-18. *Prompting Copilot Notebook (Copilot generated)*

Copilot Notebook will be useful for users who wish to provide lengthy prompts for possible answers from the AI chatbot. The generated response can be viewed without any distractions. You have to copy the content to your word processor or blogging platform like WordPress immediately. This is because the responses are not saved in the history.

Working with Copilot Plugins

Microsoft Copilot provides several plugins using which you can extend the functionality of the chatbot. As of this writing, Copilot provides eight plugins such as Search, Instacart, Kayak, Klarna, OpenTable, Phone, Shop, and Suno. The plugins are designed to perform a specific job such as cookery, travel recommendations, and shopping. Microsoft recently added a new plugin using which you can create songs via Copilot. Even though you can ask Copilot to generate content, plugins can extend the usage by offering advanced functionalities. For example, you can ask Copilot to generate songs via the Suno plugin.

For instance, you can enable a plugin, ask it to provide ingredients for a dish, and then purchase the required items directly from Instacart. Copilot plugins will enhance productivity to a large extent.

To work with Copilot plugins, you should select the plugins option from the top right-hand side. A list of available plugins will be displayed as shown in Figure 7-19. You should note that the Search plugin is enabled by default. If you disable the Search plugin, then all other plugins will be automatically deactivated. Moreover, you can only activate three plugins for a conversation.

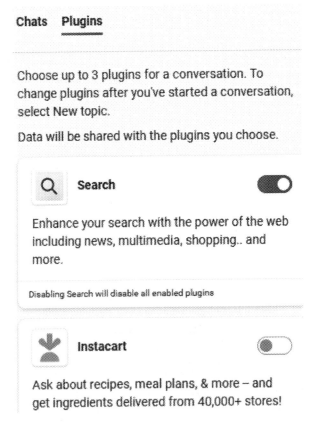

Figure 7-19. *Extending Copilot*

Let's examine the working of each plugin in detail.

Pulling Recipes via Instacart

The Instacart plugin (Figure 7-20) not only enables you to ask questions about recipes but also get delivery from local stores. To enable the plugin, you should drag the slider to the right side.

Figure 7-20. *Discover recipes*

The next step is to provide a prompt as shown in Figure 7-21.

Figure 7-21. *Find all the essentials for recipes*

The prompt here is to request Instacart to list ingredients for lemon rice. Copilot displays the results via the Instacart plugin. However, you can observe from Figure 7-22 that Copilot displays a small icon of Instacart before delivering the actual output. This indicates that Copilot has generated the required response via the Instacart plugin.

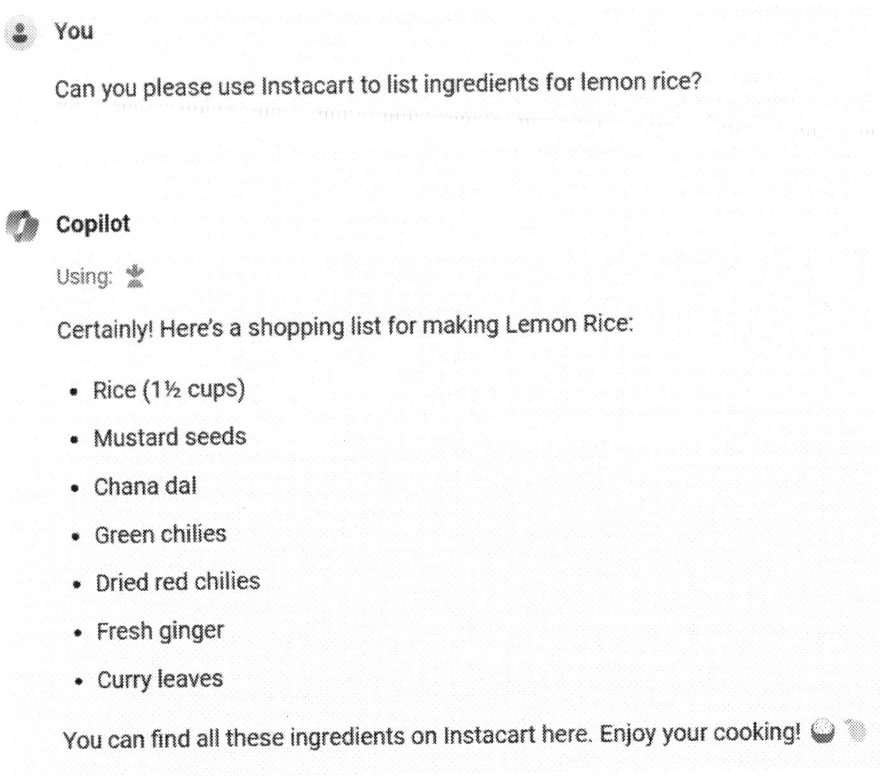

You

Can you please use Instacart to list ingredients for lemon rice?

Copilot

Using: ☟

Certainly! Here's a shopping list for making Lemon Rice:

- Rice (1½ cups)
- Mustard seeds
- Chana dal
- Green chilies
- Dried red chilies
- Fresh ginger
- Curry leaves

You can find all these ingredients on Instacart here. Enjoy your cooking! ☺ ☟

Figure 7-22. *Know the items required for lemon rice*

Copilot provides the list of ingredients and also provides a link to enable you to purchase the items. The Instacart portal lists all the ingredients required for preparing lemon rice from the Copilot-generated output. You just need to add the required items to the shopping cart from Figure 7-23.

Figure 7-23. *Purchase required items instantly*

If the original item is not available, then you will have to search for alternatives. As of this writing, the service is only available in the United States. You can also ask Instacart to provide recipe for a dish. The company maintains a huge database of various recipes, and Copilot will fetch them within minutes.

Search for Flights and Hotels via Copilot

Microsoft has integrated the Kayak plugin into Copilot, using which you can search flights, stays, and rental cars. To work with Kayak, drag the slider to activate the plugin. You can then request Copilot to provide suggestions. Let's examine a prompt as shown in Figure 7-24.

Figure 7-24. *Locate flights easily*

We are asking Kayak to provide flight suggestions from Thiruvananthapuram to Dubai on May 30. You also have to provide the date. Otherwise, Copilot will ask you to provide the date before proceeding. The resulting output looks as shown in Figure 7-25.

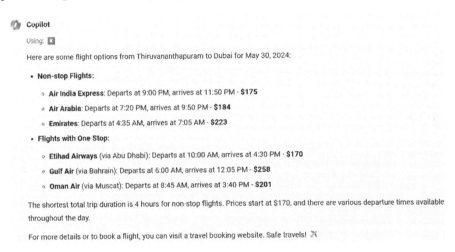

Figure 7-25. *Track flights via Copilot*

The Copilot plugin is designed to provide detailed answers, and an icon of Kayak is visible before the output. Let's ask an additional query, and the resulting output is shown in Figure 7-26.

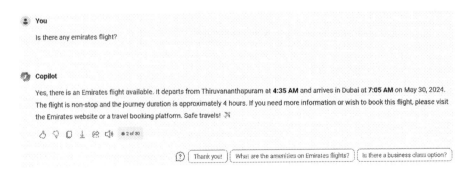

Figure 7-26. *Ask additional queries*

The Kayak plugin provides clear answers when asked about the availability of an Emirates flight on this route. Let's now ask the Copilot plugin for the presence of rental cars in the San Francisco airport as in Figure 7-27. If you ask the query in continuation, then Kayak will use the same date. You have to refresh the Copilot portal and activate the Kayak plugin if you would like to fetch answers around fresh dates.

Figure 7-27. *Find out services with Copilot*

Microsoft Copilot accurately mentions the rental car company name, location, phone, operating hours, and a thumbnail image. You can try the preceding prompt after activating the Kayak plugin and observe the result. You will be able to book a car for rent by selecting the displayed link against each entry. Even though the generated response looks accurate, you are advised to double-check the location via a search engine. AI chatbots generate responses that could vary with the actual parameters. You can explore the Kayak plugin with various prompts as per your requirements.

Price Comparison with Copilot

With a huge spike in ecommerce activities post pandemic, people are always on the lookout for new avenues to compare prices. You can now make use of the Klarna plugin to search and compare prices from a huge database of online shops. However, this service is available only in the United States.

> **Note**   Copilot can be used for advanced tasks. For instance, you can easily create flowcharts using this prompt: create a flowchart to demonstrate 2+2.

Fetch Restaurant Recommendations Quickly

There are thousands of restaurants, and it's difficult to locate a preferred place manually. Hence, you can make use of the OpenTable plugin available with Copilot. The purpose of the plugin is to provide restaurant recommendations with a direct booking link. Let's test the functioning of the plugin with a prompt as shown in Figure 7-28.

Figure 7-28. *Fetch service providers quickly*

The query is to provide restaurant recommendations in Sunnyvale, CA, and Copilot displays the response as in Figure 7-29. Currently, the plugin works only for restaurants based in the United States.

Figure 7-29. *Select a restaurant of your choice*

The plugin provides a detailed reply with information about the restaurants along with a link. You can navigate the *More info* link to know more about the restaurant, timings, and much more. Sometimes, Copilot also displays a map with the exact location of the restaurant. You will not always see the map because Microsoft Copilot is under continuous improvement.

The OpenTable plugin is a complete guide for restaurant lovers. You should make use of the plugin to fetch restaurant details if you are on a tour.

Working with Phone Plugin

Microsoft Copilot has integrated a new Phone plugin using which you can retrieve contact information. You can also read and send text messages from your Android smartphone. However, you can't work with the Copilot Phone plugin immediately after activation. You have to complete the steps to link your PC to your mobile device and vice versa. Let's look at these steps and come back to the usage of the Phone plugin.

The first step is to establish connectivity between your mobile device and your Windows 11 PC with the help of the Link to Windows app. You will be able to view the steps required to work with the Phone plugin if you request Copilot to make use of Phone to get the phone number prompt. You will see a new page with the QR code if you select the link from the Copilot response. You can also continue without the QR code by directly selecting the link displayed on the resulting page. Alternatively, you can manually download the Link to Windows app directly from Google Play Store from within your Android device. If you select the app icon on your Android device, you will be prompted to sign in with your Microsoft credentials.

The next step is to link your Windows 11 PC with your mobile device by selecting the *Go to device settings* button from the app page. You need to select the *Add a new computer* link from the *Linked computers* section. You have to navigate to the displayed URL to open the Phone Link app on your Windows 11 PC. Alternatively, you can directly open Phone Link via the Windows 11 search box to view a dashboard as shown in Figure 7-30.

Figure 7-30. *Access your phone via Windows 11*

You have to select the device platform (Android or iOS) and sign in with your Microsoft credentials. Windows 11 will display the link of linked devices on the corresponding dialog. The next step is to select your device name and proceed to provide permissions by allowing Phone, SMS, Contacts, and Storage on your mobile device. The app will provide instructions as to which permissions you should enable. You have to select the Permissions option from your Android device and manually allow the rights. The Phone Link will display a confirmation stating that your mobile device and PC are linked.

That's it. Your Android device and Windows 11 PC are linked to facilitate file access. You will be able to access files, SMS, and contacts from your Android/iOS device on your Windows 11 PC. Let's examine how to access these data with the help of the Copilot Phone plugin.

Activating Phone Copilot Plugin

To enable Copilot to fetch data from your mobile device, you should activate the Phone plugin by navigating to the Copilot dashboard. You should select the Plugins option from the top-right side and enable the Phone plugin (Figure 7-31) by scrolling down.

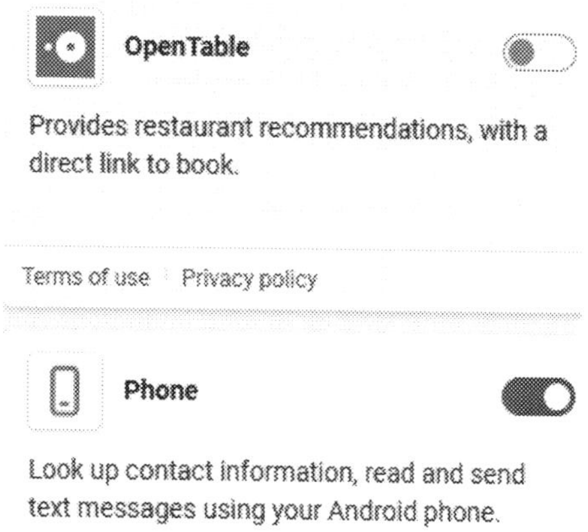

OpenTable

Provides restaurant recommendations, with a direct link to book.

Terms of use   Privacy policy

Phone

Look up contact information, read and send text messages using your Android phone.

Figure 7-31. *Activate the Phone plugin*

You can query Copilot to fetch data from your mobile device immediately after enabling the Phone plugin. You have to provide a prompt as displayed in Figure 7-32.

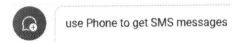

Figure 7-32. *Access SMS messages via Copilot*

Copilot will now display the list of SMS messages from your Android device as shown in Figure 7-33. The response as in Figure 7-33 will display a checked *Used: phone* entry before the results, which indicates the usage of the plugin.

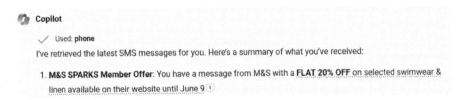

Figure 7-33. *View SMS messages directly via Copilot*

The Phone plugin can also retrieve the phone number of a contact from your mobile device. You have to provide a prompt as shown in Figure 7-34.

Figure 7-34. *Ask Copilot to display a phone number*

Copilot will immediately display the phone number from the Android mobile device as displayed in Figure 7-35.

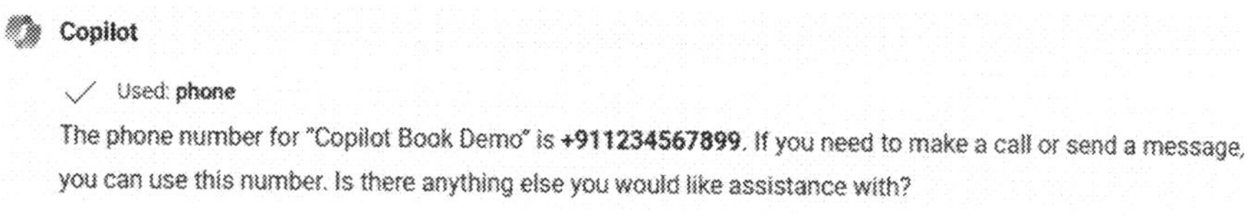

Used: **phone**

The phone number for "Copilot Book Demo" is **+911234567899**. If you need to make a call or send a message, you can use this number. Is there anything else you would like assistance with?

Figure 7-35. *Instant view of the phone number via Copilot*

In this way, you can fetch the relevant phone number and SMS messages from your linked mobile device quickly. The purpose of the Phone plugin is to enhance productivity because you can view the SMS messages directly from your Windows 11 PC. This feature will be useful in case you are charging your Android phone and would not like to use the device.

Note   If Copilot is not displaying the messages, then you should unlock your Android device to enable the chatbot to display the response.

Sometimes, the Phone link for Copilot won't work as expected because of various factors. Copilot is under continuous improvement as per user feedback. You can submit bug reports via Windows 11 Feedback Hub. You just need to press the *WIN+i* keyboard shortcut, scroll down, and select the *Give feedback* link.

Shopping with Copilot

Nowadays, you have the option to purchase millions of products from leading brands across online stores. Microsoft Copilot makes it easy for you to drill down from a huge database of products with the help of the *Shop* plugin. You should activate the plugin by dragging the slider and using a prompt as shown in Figure 7-36.

Figure 7-36. Shop easily via Copilot

The aim is to retrieve Windows 11 laptops via the Shop plugin. The Shop plugin pulled five Windows 11 laptops (see Figure 7-37) with information about price, display, processor, storage, RAM, and ports.

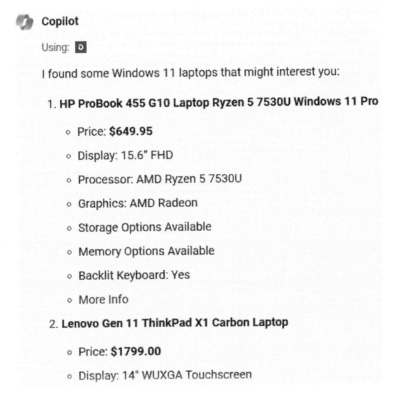

Figure 7-37. View the output delivered by the Shop plugin

If you select the *More Info* link, you will be able to navigate to the official product page on shop.app as displayed in Figure 7-38.

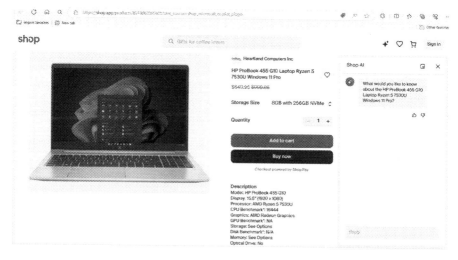

Figure 7-38. *Instant shopping simplified with Copilot*

Copilot also provides suitable suggestions toward the end of the generated content. You can search for any product based on your requirements.

Create Songs with Copilot

After the advancement of artificial intelligence over the last two years, there has been a steady rise in the creation of songs via AI. Even though AI can't replace traditional singers, you can still try to create something creative by providing suitable prompts. Microsoft has created a revolution by integrating the Suno plugin with Copilot. With the help of the Suno plugin, you can create songs. However, your song request information will be shared with Suno.

To create AI songs via Copilot, you should activate the Suno plugin by dragging the slider. You should then request Copilot to create a song by providing the required prompt. In Figure 7-39, you can see a prompt to create a song via the Suno plugin.

create a one minute melody song about nature

Figure 7-39. *Prompting Copilot to create songs*

Copilot displays the verse and chorus as shown in Figure 7-40. It will take time for the Suno plugin to create a song.

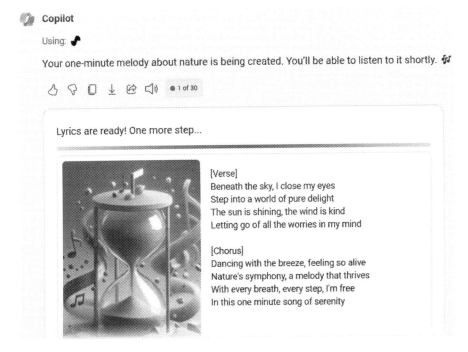

Figure 7-40. *Please wait while Copilot creates a song*

You can play the created song by selecting the Listen button. The song will play with immersive music as displayed in Figure 7-41.

 Done! Enjoy your song

[Verse]
Beneath the sky, I close my eyes
Step into a world of pure delight
The sun is shining, the wind is kind
Letting go of all the worries in my mind

[Chorus]
Dancing with the breeze, feeling so alive
Nature's symphony, a melody that thrives
With every breath, every step, I'm free
In this one minute song of serenity

Figure 7-41. Copilot playing a song (AI-generated via Copilot)

You can also share the generated song by selecting the *Share* option located below the song. The Suno-powered song can also be downloaded (Figure 7-42) by selecting the *Download* icon. You can either share the song on social media or use the song as background music during the creation of videos.

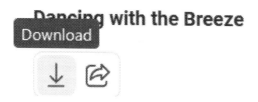

Figure 7-42. Showcase the AI song you created

Copilot displays the Suno icon before displaying the generated song. This indicates that the AI song has been created via the plugin. You can freely use the song in all your projects, including video creation and editing activities. You can create any AI song with Copilot. You just need to use the correct prompt based on your requirements. The Copilot dashboard will automatically create a history of all your communications with Copilot under the *Recents* panel.

Disclaimer   This chapter contains images that are generated via AI-enabled Microsoft Copilot. The images are only used for the sake of explanation and educational purposes.

Summary

In this chapter, you have learned the usage of the Copilot web interface in detail. The chapter examined the working of Copilot GPTs and plugins with examples. You also learned about AI image generation and Copilot Notebook. The chapter also covered the generation of songs via Copilot, including fetching SMS messages and contact information from your mobile device. The ability to create songs is a definite advantage for students, professionals, and video creators. In the next chapter, you will learn the process involved in the generation of images.

CHAPTER 8

Working with Image Creator

Microsoft released Bing Image Creator (currently Image Creator) using which you can create AI images. Bing Image Creator was unveiled shortly after the launch of Bing Chat in early 2023. However, Microsoft renamed Bing Image Creator as Image Creator after the rebranding of Bing Chat as Copilot. Image Creator works with the help of DALL·E technology, which is OpenAI's model to transform text prompts into impressive images. Microsoft also integrated the image creation module with Copilot. You can generate images directly from the Copilot in Windows, Edge, Bing, Skype and Windows app. Image Creator is a powerful product, which creates stunning AI images based on the provided prompt. In this chapter, we will examine the steps involved in the creation of images using Image Creator.

Evolution of DALL·E

Before delving deep into the usage of Image Creator, let's examine a brief history of OpenAI's DALL·E model. Microsoft has integrated this model for the generation of images. As of this writing, there are three iterations of the model such as DALL·E and DALL·E 2. The latest DALL·E 3 model

© Anand Narayanaswamy 2024
A. Narayanaswamy, *Microsoft Copilot for Windows 11*, Inside Copilot,
https://doi.org/10.1007/979-8-8688-0583-7_8

is infused with several new features and improvements. OpenAI has employed advanced machine learning and deep learning techniques in the development of DALL·E. The model can generate accurate digital images from natural language descriptions called prompts.

OpenAI released the first version of DALL·E in January 2021 followed by the DALL·E 2 model in April 2022. The company natively released DALL·E 3 along with ChatGPT Plus and ChatGPT Enterprise in October 2023. Moreover, the OpenAI API and Labs platform was also made available in November 2023. Microsoft has integrated the DALL·E model in Image Creator (formerly Bing Image Creator).

DALL·E makes use of a modified version of GPT-3 to generate images. DALL·E 2 was designed to generate realistic and natural images with high-resolution support. OpenAI issued beta invitations to over one million waitlisted individuals on July 20, 2022. The system was designed in such a way that DALL·E could generate a fixed number of images for free in the form of credits. The user needs to buy additional credits. The DALL·E 2 waitlist policy was removed on September 28, 2023, but the company announced the arrival of the DALL·E 3 advanced imaging model. DALL·E 3 was developed with nuance and detailed AI images compared to the previous iterations.

OpenAI released the DALL·E 2 API in November 2023, which enables developers to integrate the imaging model into their own applications. The Designer app and Bing Image Creator tool were shipped with the DALL·E model, which was widely accepted by creators. The API is designed to work on a cost-per-image basis based on the image resolution. OpenAI started to add watermarks to DALL·E-generated images starting February 2024. The watermark contains metadata in the Coalition for Content Provenance and Authenticity (C2PA) standard as prompted by the Content Authenticity Initiative.

DALL·E is a multimodal implementation of GPT-3 with 12 billion parameters, which intelligently swaps text for pixels. The model is aggressively trained based on text-image pairs from the Web. The transformer model input is a sequence of tokenized image captions coupled with tokenized image patches. The generated images comprise a 256×256 RGB, divided into 32×32 patches of 4×4, respectively. The patches are converted by a discrete variational autoencoder to a token. Initially, the images were generated from a list of 32,768 captions that were randomly selected from the dataset. However, OpenAI is constantly training the model and corresponding dataset to enable DALL·E to deliver stunning pictures. DALL·E 2 makes use of 3.5 billion parameters alongside a diffusion model based on CLIP image embeddings.

DALL·E is capable of generating images in multiple styles such as photorealistic imagery, painting works, and emojis. The model also emits a broad understanding of visual and design trends. OpenAI has developed DALL·E to generate images for several descriptions from various viewpoints. DALL·E 3 is designed to work with advanced prompts with detailed accuracy when compared with the previous counterparts. Even though DALL·E 3 is available with ChatGPT Plus, you can experience the model via Image Creator from Microsoft Designer.

Understanding Image Creator

After the launch of Bing Chat in early 2023, Microsoft launched Bing Image Creator (currently Image Creator) which uses the DALL·E imaging model. Currently, AI images are generated via the DALL·E 3 model. The purpose of Image Creator is to create stunning images based on the provided prompt.

Tip   You can create images using Microsoft Designer, Copilot in Windows (preview), Microsoft Edge, Bing, Skype, Copilot Web, and Copilot Windows apps, including Microsoft Copilot Android and iOS apps. You can also generate images, stickers, avatars, icons, emojis and much more using Microsoft Designer Android and iOS apps.

To work with Image Creator, you should navigate to `www.bing.com/images/create`. The dashboard looks as shown in Figure 8-1. You should note that the screenshot mentions Designer, which is currently renamed as Image Creator. Moreover, the Copilot logo has been replaced with Microsoft Bing. The appearance of the Image Creator home page could change periodically.

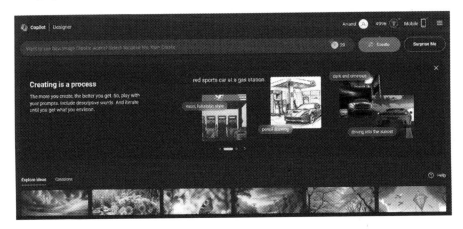

Figure 8-1. *Create stunning images with Image Creator*

The next step is to provide a suitable prompt inside the *Want to see how Image Creator works?* textbox to enable Image Creator to generate images. Alternatively, you can also select the *Surprise Me* button to enable Image Creator to automatically generate prompts. You will have to select the button several times to view a prompt of your choice. Image Creator displays a progress indicator in three dots for a few seconds while it identifies a suitable prompt.

Let's check out how Image Creator generates images with the automated prompt: *gorgeous abandoned medieval mansion in a fairytale forest*. You have to select the *Create* button to enable Image Creator to generate images. The creator displays a splash page as shown in Figure 8-2.

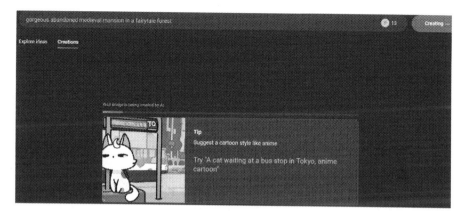

Figure 8-2. *Image Creator waiting indicator*

Note   The number specified adjacent to the textbox indicates daily boosts. You will be able to create images even if you run out of daily boosts, but the image creation process will take longer than expected.

You will see four AI images upon successful completion of the image generation. Image Creator reveals the information that the images are powered by the DALL·E 3 model. This model is capable of creating powerful and stunning images when compared with the previous counterparts.

Note   The images zoom in as you hover your mouse over them. Try it. It will be an interesting experience.

The look and feel of the images will change when you attempt the same prompt using Image Creator. Copilot will not generate the same image every time because of the various factors involved with the model. You should note that AI technology is under constant change and development. Hence, the responses produced by Copilot will vary depending on the location. Even if the image generated by the creator is provided here, you won't view the same output. Hence, you should try to generate the images as per the preceding prompt by following the instructions. You can also provide a prompt of your choice and requirement to enable Image Creator to create stunning visuals.

If you select an image, you will see an enlarged version as in Figure 8-3 with details about the resolution, image format, and much more.

Figure 8-3. *Decide what to do with the image*

You can send the image over social media by selecting the *Share* button. Image Creator displays the URL along with the *Copy* button as shown in Figure 8-4.

Figure 8-4. *Showcase your AI image*

The button changes the caption to *Copied* upon selection. The URL will be too long that you will not be able to remember or type it manually on the web browser. Hence, you can add the image to Image Creator Collections by selecting the *Save* button. You will see a pop-up menu as in Figure 8-5.

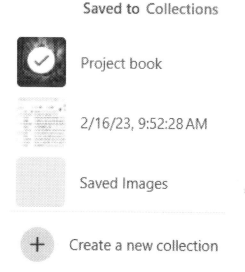

Figure 8-5. Collections entry point

You can create a new collection by selecting the *Create a new collection* option. You will see a user interface as shown in Figure 8-6. The main purpose behind the creation of collections is that you will be able to easily access the images via www.bing.com/saves.

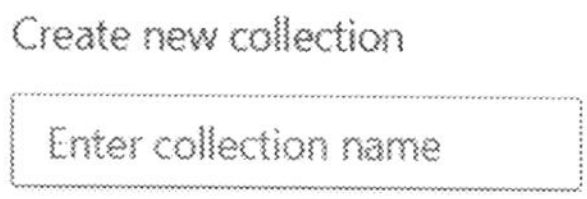

Figure 8-6. Easily create a new collection

A tick mark will be visible upon entering the collection name, which will appear on the pop-up dialog as displayed in Figure 8-7. You have to select the mouse pointer over the tick mark icon to save the image into the collection.

Create new collection
copilot book

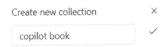

Figure 8-7. *Collection successfully created*

The image will be saved to the collections, and a confirmation pop-up will appear as shown in Figure 8-8.

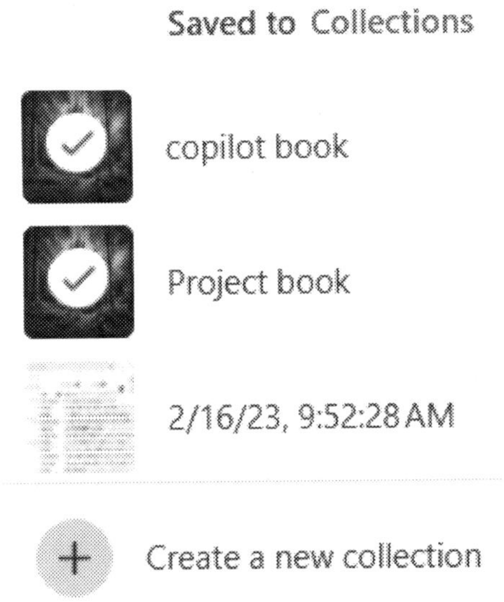
Saved to Collections
copilot book
Project book
2/16/23, 9:52:28 AM
Create a new collection

Figure 8-8. *View all collections in a flash*

You can view the saved image inside the Collections dashboard by selecting the *Open collections portal* icon as shown in Figure 8-9.

Figure 8-9. *Open the Collections dashboard*

If you select the icon, you will see the saved image inside the Collections as shown in Figure 8-10.

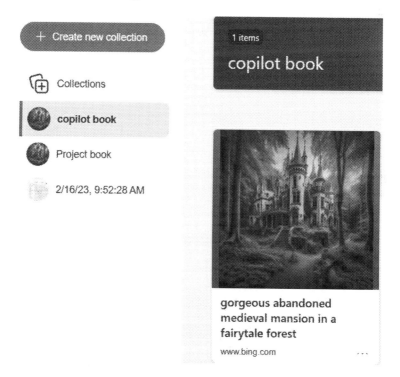

Figure 8-10. *Collections portal in action*

The Collections portal also enables you to add notes upon selecting the *Add note* option from the top navigation panel. You can provide the relevant content inside the sticky note as shown in Figure 8-11.

Figure 8-11. *Create notes inside the Collections portal*

In addition to saving the generated image using the *Download* button as we examined in Figure 8-3, you can also edit the image directly on the cloud. You can easily personalize the image by adding filters and other properties by clicking the *Customize* button. The Microsoft Designer dashboard will be displayed on the screen using which you can perform all the required editing work as shown in Figure 8-12.

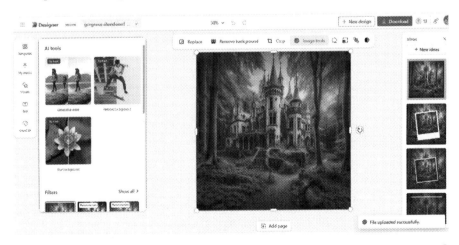

Figure 8-12. *Microsoft Designer dashboard in action*

> **Note**   Microsoft Designer (`https://designer.microsoft.com`) is an exclusive app using which you can easily create images, stickers, avatars, invitations, icons, emojis, clip art and image collages as well as remove background from images.

Generating Images Using Own Prompts

You can also provide your own prompts to create images with Image Creator. Let's give a prompt such as *A garden with water fountain surrounded by yellow flowers*. The creator generates four images along with a disclaimer statement that the images are generated by AI. You should be aware that Image Creator doesn't create four images always. This is mainly due to the nature of AI technology. You have to click the Create button and wait until Image Creator generates the images.

If you select any one of the generated images, an enlarged version will display along with other options that are the same as we discussed earlier. We observed that Image Creator accurately generated the images with a waterfall and yellow flowers upon our testing. You can play with various prompts as per your requirements. You should also note that the creator generates different images upon each attempt because of the AI technology.

Viewing AI Images

The Image Creator dashboard displays select images that are generated by users. These images are curated by the Microsoft Copilot team. You can scroll down the dashboard to view the AI images that are preloaded by the creator. Moreover, the rotating carousel also displays stunning images that are ready for immediate consumption. You will see a large-sized image with the option to download for your usage upon selection of an image from the dashboard.

Tip   You can generate AI images via Image Creator in Microsoft Paint. However, this feature is currently limited to users in the United States, France, the UK, Australia, Canada, Italy, and Germany.

Alternatively, you can view the images created by Image Creator by selecting the *Creations* tab. The creator displays the latest generated image. You can view all the generated images using prompts manually by selecting the relevant image from the *Recent* panel. You can use the scroll bar to navigate the images that you have created. Even though the creator generates four images for a prompt, there are instances where it renders three images. It all depends upon the prompt and the way the back-end engine works.

You should note that Image Creator won't generate any results if your prompt is harmful and offensive. Microsoft has applied adequate safety precautions to safeguard the interests of the general community, including kids.

Caution   See the Image Creator Terms: `www.bing.com/new/termsofuseimagecreator`.

You should make sure not to violate any content policy terms to avoid suspension and cancellation of your Microsoft account. Image Creator has been developed to enable you to generate awesome creations based on the prompt. You should make use of the tool responsibly, and you are only responsible for any harm caused to anyone. You can make use of Image Creator for your personal consumption such as for your blogs and social media. You can generate a featured image for your blog post very easily just by giving the relevant context.

Disclaimer   You should note that the AI-generated images in Figures 8-1, 8-2, 8-3, 8-10, 8-11, and 8-12 have no resemblance to any living humans or properties. The images are generated by Microsoft's Image Creator and are used only for educational purposes.

Summary

In this chapter, you have learned the process involved in the creation of images using Image Creator. You only need to provide the required prompt, and the creator will take care of the rest of the work. You can even share and download images, including the ability to edit them quickly by adding effects and filters. In the next chapter, you will learn about the working of Microsoft Designer in detail.

CHAPTER 9

Working with Microsoft Designer

Microsoft Designer is a complete and robust Copilot-enabled AI design application. You can easily create AI images, stickers, designs, invitations, wallpapers, avatars, and icons, including the ability to remove background. The app has been upgraded with new features such as image restyling, collage, and greeting card creator, including instant background removal and generative eraser. The Designer tool intelligently suggests unique designs and also provides personalized recommendations. You can even add filters and adjust brightness, contrast, and other related settings to your images. You will be able to create stunning designs even without any basic design knowledge. In this chapter, you will learn the usage of modules included with Microsoft Designer in detail.

Overview of Microsoft Designer

Microsoft Designer leverages DALL·E 3 technology to generate stunning and powerful images. You just need to have a creative mindset so that you can provide the relevant prompt. You can customize and refine the generated images. It's possible to add motion effects and filters to your design. Moreover, you can convert a simple post to Instagram reel or story

© Anand Narayanaswamy 2024
A. Narayanaswamy, *Microsoft Copilot for Windows 11*, Inside Copilot,
https://doi.org/10.1007/979-8-8688-0583-7_9

with several attractive elements. Microsoft has integrated Generative AI into the Designer app by adding Generative Erase. The Designer makes use of the Segment Anything Model (SAM), which enables users to select specific areas they would like to remove from an image. The upcoming Generative Fill functionality automatically fills objects within an image or background. You just require creativity and imagination. If you would like to expand your image irrespective of border, you can use the upcoming Generative Expand model powered by the DALL·E 3 model.

Microsoft Designer has been developed in such a way that even a beginner can work with the app easily. You need not have to be a skilled designer to create intuitive, rich, and attractive designs. You can create AI images, stickers, invitations, digital postcards, and social media posts. The Designer is in the preview stage, and the product team is working continuously to improve the features included with the product. You can submit feedback in case you face any problems by selecting the *Send feedback to Microsoft* icon located on the top right-hand side as shown in Figure 9-1.

Send feedback to Microsoft

Figure 9-1. *Report bug fixes instantly*

Microsoft evaluates Designer experience with a combination of user engagement methods. This includes accessing the performance during the preview phase, directing user interviews, and dissecting the product feedback database. According to Microsoft, this user-centric approach will pave the way for not only qualitative insights but also objective measurements. The performance of the Designer app will be measured by taking into account various factors such as user engagement rates, usability metrics, user interface performance, and feedback gathering. Microsoft has been adding new features and modules to the Designer app regularly.

Working with Microsoft Designer

To create images, stickers, designs, invitations, avatars, and icons with Microsoft Designer, you should navigate to https://designer.microsoft.com. A dashboard will be displayed as shown in Figure 9-2. You should note that Microsoft Designer is currently available only in the English language. However, there is a possibility that Microsoft could provide support for multiple languages in the future.

Figure 9-2. *Kick-start your design journey*

The carousel placed on the Microsoft Designer home page enables you to create images, greeting cards, collages, social posts, invitations, stickers, wallpapers, monograms, backgrounds, avatars, and icons. You can quickly access modules like background remover, Generative Erase, image framing, and much more by selecting the *Edit with AI* tab from the Designer dashboard.

Note   The appearance of the Microsoft Designer home page could change periodically.

If you scroll down the Microsoft Designer home page, you will see options as in Figure 9-3 for the creation of images, personalized avatars, greeting cards, wallpapers, invitations, and much more.

Figure 9-3. *Select what you want to create*

The options displayed on the Microsoft Designer home page change upon each page refresh. You should read the description and proceed further with your tasks. Moreover, the Designer app displays prompt templates under each heading. You will be able to quickly create stunning graphics by selecting a relevant template of your choice. If you point your mouse over an image template, then the relevant prompt will appear. You will have an option to change the prompt before you proceed to generate visuals.

Creating Images

To create images, you should select the *Images* option from the Microsoft Designer dashboard. You will see a screen as shown in Figure 9-4.

Figure 9-4. Start generating AI images here

Alternatively, you can also provide a suitable prompt as per your choice in the search box located on the top of the Microsoft Designer dashboard. You will see a series of options as shown in Figure 9-5. You have to provide a prompt and select an option. For example, you can use a prompt like *A beautiful lake surrounded by flowers* and select the Images option. The Designer app automatically generates images for you.

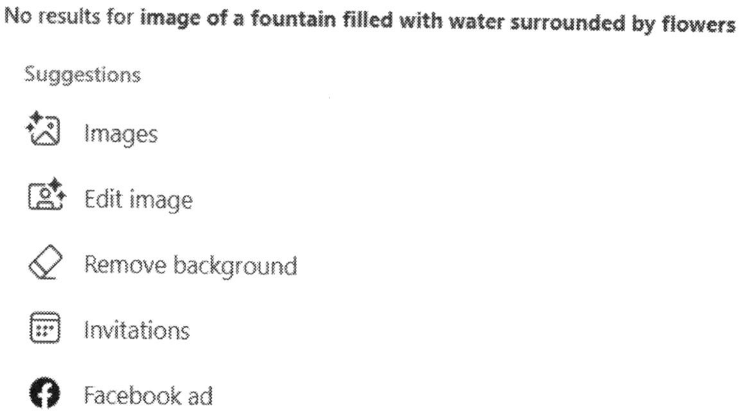

No results for **image of a fountain filled with water surrounded by flowers**

Suggestions

- Images
- Edit image
- Remove background
- Invitations
- Facebook ad

Figure 9-5. Intelligent suggestions upon entering a prompt

If you select the Images option from the Microsoft Designer home page, you will see a new dashboard using which you can create images. The Image Creator provides several predefined prompts with previews, which you can use to learn the usage of the tool. A new set of image previews and prompts will be displayed upon refreshing the page. If you hover over the preview, you will be able to know the prompt description as shown in Figure 9-6.

Figure 9-6.   *Point your mouse to view the prompt*

If you click the preview placeholder, you will be able to edit the selected portions of the prompt as displayed in Figure 9-7.

Figure 9-7.   *Edit prompt intelligently*

You can also modify the entire relevant prompt by selecting the *Edit entire prompt* option as displayed in Figure 9-8.

An image of an ice cream waffle cone with scoops of purple, pink, and yellow ice cream inside. The cone should be balancing on its tip with small dribbles and splats of ice cream underneath. The ice cream should look like it is starting to explode with liquid splashes flying off the top of the cone. The background should be a soft purple gradient color with even studio lighting.

Figure 9-8. *Modify prompt completely*

If you are satisfied with the prompt, you should select the *Generate* button to enable Image Creator to render the image. The app will display four blue-colored square placeholders, where the generated images will appear as shown in Figure 9-9. You should note that the image generation process takes time depending upon the speed of your Internet connectivity and other external AI factors. Moreover, a new set of four images will appear upon each refresh because of the nature of AI technology.

Figure 9-9. *View the variations of AI-generated images*

Let's try to create another image from the predefined prompts. A new set of four images will appear on the screen. If you select an image, you will see a window with a larger preview (Figure 9-10) along with the options for downloading and editing the relevant image. You can also navigate to another image by selecting the navigation arrows placed on the left and right sides.

A full frame poster with dots, stars, and lines in bright, saturated colors in a pop art style. The lines should be narrow in the center and widen as they extend to the edge of the canvas. The background should be kitschy and include polka dots and zig zag lines. The design should include text in a white cloud shape reading, "Pop!" and "Wow!"

Figure 9-10. *Decide what you want to do with the AI image*

You can make use of the image on your blog or share them on social media by selecting the *Download* option. If you select the *Edit* option, a comprehensive design editor page will appear as displayed in Figure 9-11.

Figure 9-11. *Edit your designs on the cloud*

You can add filters, texts, and other elements with the help of the Designer dashboard. The Designer dashboard includes several options that are located on the left and right sides in addition to the top bar.

You can also adjust the brightness, contrast, sharpness, saturation, and temperature levels of the active image. You will be able to view the change instantly upon dragging the sliders. You can also remove background and crop images easily as well as add text to your images.

Create Images with Your Prompts

You can also create images using your prompts. The first step is to navigate to https://designer.microsoft.com/image-creator. You should provide the required prompt like *Generate an image of a waterfall surrounded by trees* inside the *Description* section and select the size according to your requirements.

Alternatively, you can provide the required prompt inside the textbox provided on the Microsoft Designer home page and select the required option of your choice. Let's provide a prompt as shown in Figure 9-12.

Generate an image of a waterfall surrounded by trees

Figure 9-12. *Prompting with Microsoft Designer*

The next step is to select the desired size by selecting the Size option. The Designer app displays three design options, namely, Square, Portrait, and Wide. The final step is to select the *Generate* button to enable Microsoft Designer to generate the relevant image. The app displays a blue-colored progress indicator in four squares in different variations. If you try the abovementioned prompt using the Designer app, then you will be able to view stunning visuals according to our prompt. The image creation process is the same even if you attempt a new prompt. The ability to pick a size of your choice is a definite advantage. As explained earlier, you can easily modify the generated image by selecting the *Edit* option.

Using Microsoft Designer Dashboard

Microsoft Designer comes with a robust editor using which you can modify your image effectively. You can also add impressive elements using the various options inside the editor. The Designer ships with plenty of templates, which you can use for your projects. You can also search using keywords to locate a template of your choice. Firstly, you should select the *Templates* icon from the top left-side navigation panel and select a template based on your requirement.

You can upload your own media to the Designer app from various sources by selecting the *My media* icon as shown in Figure 9-13. Moreover, the Designer app automatically syncs with OneDrive and displays all the latest images.

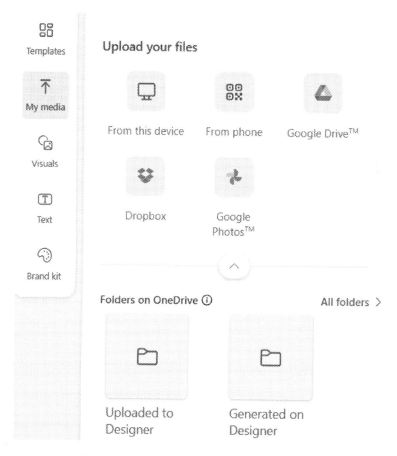

Figure 9-13. Upload files from various sources

You will have to grant the required permission if you would like to use media content from Google Drive or Google Photos. If you select Google Drive, you will see a dialog prompting you to establish connectivity by selecting the *Connect Google Drive* button.

The *Visuals* option in Microsoft Designer enables you to add several attractive shapes and icons to your image as displayed in Figure 9-14. You can add shapes, illustrations, background photos/videos, summer icons, and much more. The possibilities are endless, and it's up to you to decide the relevant visual element of your choice. You should also judge the selection as per your project requirements.

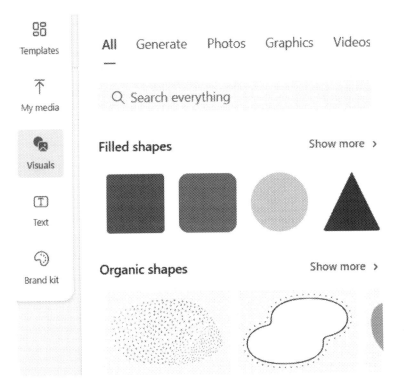

Figure 9-14. *Pick elements and add*

The Designer app dashboard displays three or four shapes, but you will see more upon selecting the *Show more* option. You can add attractive text content and options as shown in Figure 9-15 to the active image by selecting the *Text* option. You can adjust the location and size after adding the relevant selection to the image editor.

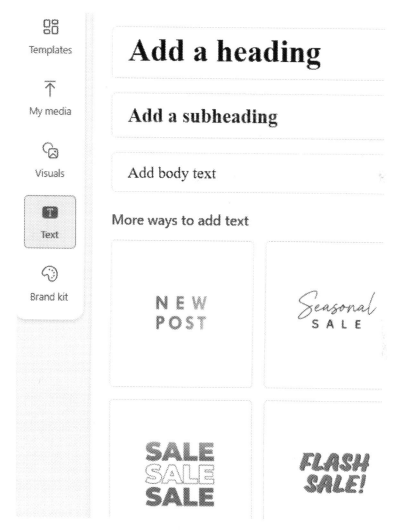

Figure 9-15. *Add a text of your choice*

You need to double-click the default text inside the placeholder and add the required content. Previously, Microsoft also integrated the Copilot API into the text module. If you provide the relevant text inside the top textbox after selecting the *Text* icon from the left-side navigation, the tool will generate text content accordingly. Let's check out how the tool displays the various options after entering the word *Welcome*. Microsoft Designer provides several automated AI-based font options for the active text item as shown in Figure 9-16. You have to experiment with each and decide accordingly based on your project requirements.

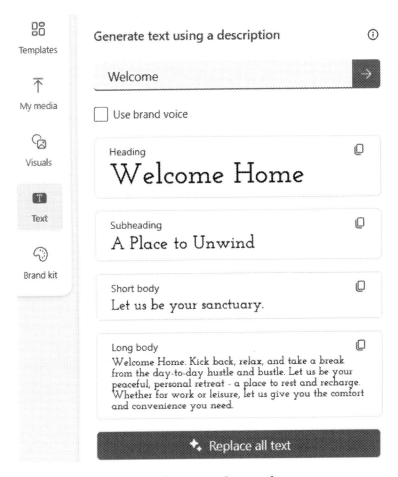

Figure 9-16. *Select a font style as per the needs*

If you select an option, the relevant text design will appear inside the image editor. There is no need to drag and drop inside the editing window. The font size can be increased by dragging the placeholders.

Note   The AI-enabled text options are not available now but could appear in the future. You are requested to check the Microsoft Designer editor to verify the presence of this functionality.

You can also make use of the font bar (Figure 9-17) located on top of the image and adjust the parameters. However, if you click outside the editor, the textbox loses focus and the front bar will disappear.

Figure 9-17. *Apply fonts easily*

If you select the active image on the Microsoft Designer editor, you will see options as shown in Figure 9-18.

Figure 9-18. *Perform Advanced Tasks Quickly*

You can swap the image by selecting the *Replace* option from the top navigation bar. You will see options as displayed in Figure 9-19. While the Image gallery provides several stock images, icons, and illustrations, the My media icon enables you to upload your objects and icons, including images.

Figure 9-19. *Add external images*

177

You can also remove background or crop an image by selecting the appropriate options as per your requirement. If you select the *Image tools* option, you will see AI tools such as Generative Erase and background removal, including the ability to blur the background. You can perform all the work from within the image editor. For instance, you can remove certain portions of an image using the Generative Erase functionality.

Microsoft Designer also provides attractive filters, which you can view by selecting the *Image tools* option. The relevant filters appear inside the AI tools panel under the Filters section. You can select the *Show all* option to view all the available filters.

Note   The appearance of the filters depends upon the active image inside the Microsoft Designer editor.

You need to select the desired filter to apply it to the active image. You can also convert a color image to black and white and much more. The Filters pane automatically shows a small preview of how the original image will look like upon applying the desired filter.

The Designer app is bundled with powerful features. Hence, a person with a creative mindset will be able to leverage the full potential of all the tools included with the app. Microsoft has developed the tool in such a way that even a beginner will be able to learn all the aspects without any assistance.

Generating Social Posts

Microsoft Designer also enables you to generate social posts based on the provided prompt. Previously, this feature was named Ideas. You can create stunning graphics for your upcoming book, product, and much more based on a single prompt.

The first step is to select the *Social posts* icon located on the Microsoft Designer home page. You will see a screen as shown in Figure 9-20. You will also view several image prompts with the relevant default content on the *Try a prompt* navigation panel.

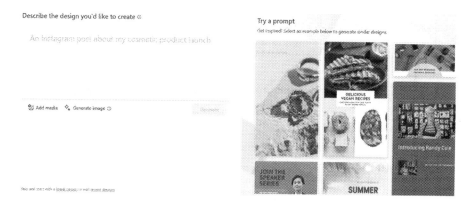

Figure 9-20. *Create images based on ideas*

You have to mention the kind of design you would like to create. You can also add media from your PC or ask Microsoft Designer to generate an image using a suitable prompt.

Let's try to create an Instagram post using Microsoft Designer as shown in Figure 9-21. You can also upload media from your device to create graphics. The Social posts dashboard also provides attractive animated prompts, which you can make use of to jump-start your design work.

Figure 9-21. *Provide idea prompts here*

A splash screen with the caption *Generating designs for you* will display while the app creates the designs. You have to pick a design and select the *Customise design* button, which appears below the generated social posts. Microsoft Designer also displays automated prompt suggestions based on your original prompt as shown in Figure 9-22, which you can make use of to generate accurate social posts.

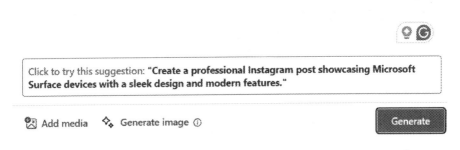

Figure 9-22. *Automated prompt suggestion helps*

You will see a list of generated social posts as shown in Figure 9-23. You can scroll down to view additional designs. Microsoft Designer generates new social posts if you repeat the generation of designs using the same prompt. The AI technology is designed to generate new responses in the form of text, images, and videos.

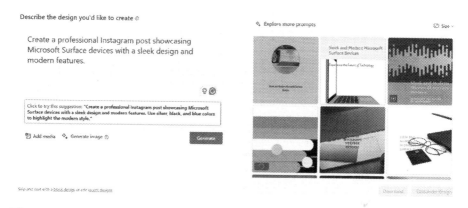

Figure 9-23. *Pick a suitable design as per your requirement*

The next step is to select a design and then click the *Customise design* button. The selected design appears inside the Microsoft Designer dashboard as shown in Figure 9-24. You can add elements such as shapes, text, and other media content.

Figure 9-24. *Modify the selected design*

You can either add additional pages (see Figure 9-25) or duplicate the existing page by selecting the *Add page* button located below the design. You can make use of the design ideas displayed on the right side for additional pages.

Figure 9-25. *Paginate your design*

Creating Stickers

Microsoft Designer also includes a dedicated module for the creation of stickers. The first step is to select the *Stickers* option by navigating to https://designer.microsoft.com. In Figure 9-26, you can observe the Sticker Creator dashboard.

Figure 9-26. *Impress your friends with stickers*

The dashboard displays a preview of several stickers. If you point your mouse over the stickers, then you will be able to view the relevant prompt. The remaining steps are identical to that of the Image Creator we saw previously. The system creates four stickers upon selecting the *Generate* button similar to that of the Image Creator. Like in the case of the images, stickers will also change upon each AI request.

If you select one sticker, a pop-up window will open using which you can download the generated sticker. You can also open the sticker inside the Microsoft Designer dashboard by selecting the *Edit* option. You can apply filters, elements, text, and other properties from the Microsoft Designer dashboard as displayed in Figure 9-27.

Figure 9-27. Modify the sticker inside the Designer dashboard

You can download the sticker by selecting the *Download* button after the completion of the editing process. The file can be downloaded in PNG, JPEG, and PDF file formats. You can also copy the image or deliver the relevant image to your phone as shown in Figure 9-28.

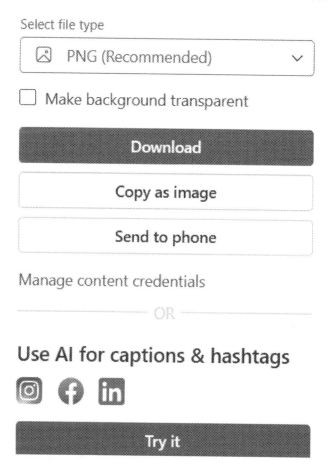

Figure 9-28. *Download and share*

Note   In case you are not satisfied with the sticker or observe any error, then you can send feedback to the product team by selecting the *Send feedback* option.

The Designer app suggests PNG as the recommended format, which produces high-quality images. The Designer app also provides the ability to use AI for the creation of captions and hashtags. Moreover, you can manage content credentials by including the required parameters.

Note   Try to create a sticker by using your own prompt – *Create a funny smiling sticker for sharing on WhatsApp group.*

If you select a sticker, you will be able to modify the sticker via the *Edit* option as discussed earlier. You can easily generate stickers by providing a suitable prompt according to your requirements.

Creating Awesome Greeting Cards

Microsoft Designer enables you to create stunning greeting cards based on a simple prompt. It's easy to create immersive greeting cards with the help of this module. You can provide prompts according to the relevant occasion.

Note   You can edit photos in Microsoft Designer via Photos app. You should select *Edit an image in Designer online* option from the navigation toolbar after opening the relevant image in the Photos app.

The first step is to select the Greeting cards option from the Microsoft Designer home page. The Greeting cards editor is displayed as shown in Figure 9-29. You can select the Greeting card templates and ideas dynamically available on the Designer dashboard. Alternatively, you can provide a new prompt by clicking the description area.

Explore ideas
About
Congrats
THANK YOU

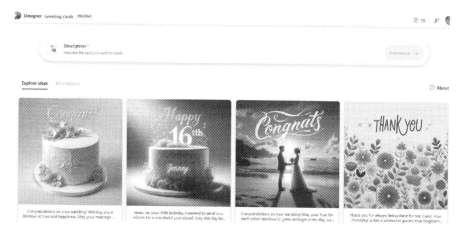

Figure 9-29. *Create greeting cards for various occasions*

If you select a Greeting card template, you will be able to modify the prompt from the displayed prompt editing panel. You can provide the desired values inside the activated textbox as shown in Figure 9-30. You can also edit the prompt in full by selecting the *Edit entire prompt* option.

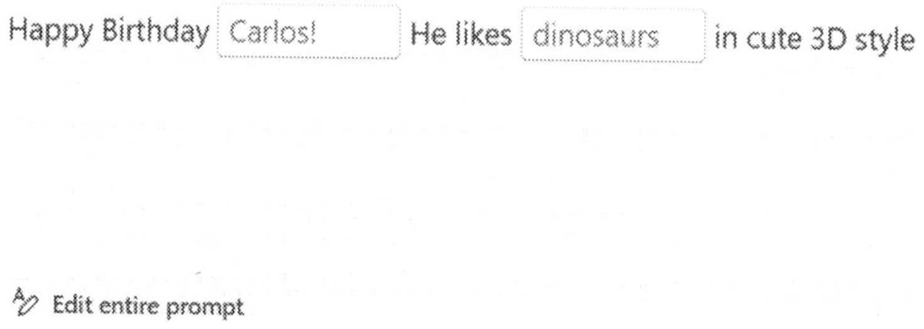

Happy Birthday
Carlos!
He likes
dinosaurs
in cute 3D style
Edit entire prompt

Figure 9-30. *Prompting to create greeting cards*

Finally, you should select the *Generate* button, and the Designer automatically creates four variations of the card. If you select a generated greeting card, it will open as an envelope and will be visible on the screen. You can easily download the card for social media purposes. Sometimes, you will not be able to download the generated greeting card because of various reasons. You can try again later to download the card.

You can modify the text content by selecting the *Edit text* button located on the top-right side of the selected greeting card. An editing placeholder will appear on the screen, and you can directly provide a suitable text. The caption of the *Download* button changes to *Looks good,* which you should select if you are satisfied with the new content. You can then save the greeting card to your PC by selecting the *Download* button. If you press the *Esc* key, the Designer will reveal the other three greeting cards. You can download them as well in case you are not satisfied with the previous card.

Collage Creator

Microsoft Designer includes a handy Collage Creator functionality. You can beautify old images to create a single impressive image, also named collage, with the help of AI. Imagine you located vacation photos with your office colleagues. You can easily turn them into collages using the Designer app. You can add elements and style to create an impressive social media experience.

The first step is to select the *Collages* option from the Designer home page. The Collage Creator dashboard as shown in Figure 9-31 will be displayed upon selecting the option.

Figure 9-31. *Create a fun collage with Microsoft Designer*

Microsoft Designer displays a fresh set of collage templates upon each refresh. You can upload a maximum of ten photos per collage. You have an option to select a deserted style according to your requirements. The Collage Creator includes several amazing styles as shown in Figure 9-32.

Figure 9-32. *Apply styles to your collage easily*

Let's deploy a few scenic photos into the Collage Creator via Figure 9-33 and observe the result. You can upload photos from your phone, Google Drive/Photos, and Dropbox by selecting the *Add images* button.

Figure 9-33. *Fill your collage with images*

The tool loads all the photos from OneDrive automatically and can be completely viewed by selecting the Media on OneDrive panel. The uploaded photos will be visible on the *Media on Designer* panel after uploading the images.

To create a collage, you have to manually select the relevant images and click the *Select* button. The selected photos will appear inside the Images panel. You can add objects or themes to your collage by selecting the Elements tab. The Collage Creator also comes with several styles, but it's not compulsory to add them into your collage project. The final step is to select the *Generate* button, which creates the collage using the selected photos and other parameters.

The Collage Creator generates four different variations of the collage. You will be able to view an enlarged collage upon selecting any of the generated collages. You can either download or modify the collage by selecting the *Download* and *Edit* buttons, respectively. You can add shapes, icons, text, and other items via the Microsoft Designer dashboard, which will be visible upon selecting the *Edit* button.

Creating Invitations

Do you want to create an invitation for a family party? Microsoft Designer is here to your rescue because you can create stunning invitations on the fly. The first step is to select the *Invitations* option from the Designer home page. You will see Invitations dashboard as shown in Figure 9-34.

Figure 9-34. *Create greeting cards for various occasions*

Like in the case of image creation, you have to provide a suitable prompt. You can either select any one of the available prompts or provide your prompt by selecting *Description*. If you select a prompt from the Explore Ideas section, you will see the corresponding prompt with placeholders for providing data as shown in Figure 9-35.

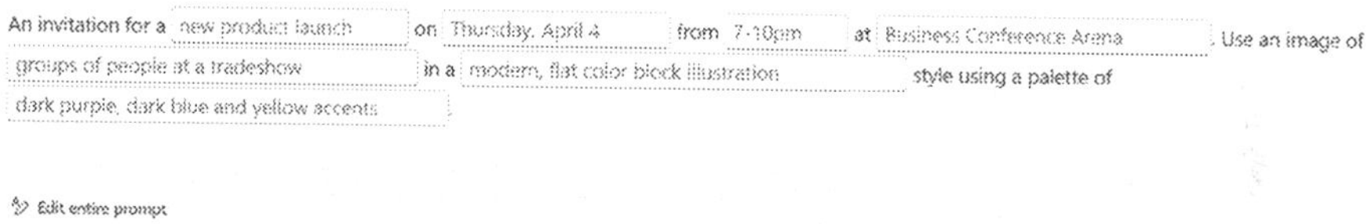

An invitation for a
new product launch
on
Thursday, April 4
from
7-10pm
at
Business Conference Arena
. Use an image of
groups of people at a tradeshow
in a
modern, flat color block illustration
style using a palette of
dark purple, dark blue and yellow accents
Edit entire prompt

Figure 9-35. *Practice prompting to create awesome greetings*

If you are satisfied with the prompt, you should select the *Generate* button. Microsoft Designer creates invitations with three different variations. You should note that the total number of creations will vary depending on the various factors related to AI. You will see an enlarged version of the invite upon selection of *Download* and *Edit* buttons. You will see two options as shown in Figure 9-36 upon selecting the *Download* button.

Download
Send to phone
Copy image

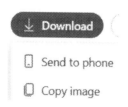

Figure 9-36. *Download in various ways*

The selected invitation appears inside the Microsoft Designer dashboard, which you can spruce up with fonts, elements, and filters. In this way, you can create invitations for any occasion by adding your preferences.

Generating Wallpapers

With the latest upgrade, you can easily create wallpapers via the Designer app. Firstly, you should select the *Wallpapers* option from the Designer home page. You will see options for providing a prompt and size along with several attractive prompt templates as shown in Figure 9-37. You can view additional prompts upon scrolling.

Figure 9-37. Decorate your system with AI wallpaper

You have to provide a suitable prompt and select a size according to your preference. The wallpaper will be created upon selecting the Generate button. You can generate wallpapers in square, portrait, and wide formats, respectively.

Microsoft Designer provides an ability for the creation of monograms. You can create interesting images by overlapping multiple letters in such a way as to form one symbol. Normally, monograms are created by combining the initials of a specific entity and can be used as a logo. You will see the Monogram dashboard upon selecting the option from the Designer app. The monogram will be created upon providing the prompt and size. You can either download or edit the generated monogram. In addition to monograms, you can also generate coloring book pages, backgrounds, avatars, and icons using Microsoft Designer. You should provide a suitable prompt and select the size according to your requirements. Microsoft Designer provides an ability to create designs using your own images for various purposes. You should select *Design from scratch* option from the Designer home page, choose the relevant blank template and add your image. You can add elements like photos, shapes, illustrations, icons, videos, and text as per your project requirements.

Advanced Microsoft Designer Features

In addition to images, social posts, stickers, greeting cards, collages, and much more, Microsoft Designer also includes advanced features. These include background removal, Generative Eraser, image restyler, and image framing. In this section, you will learn the usage of each of the advanced Designer modules.

Remove Image Background Quickly

Do you have an image with a distracting background? You can easily remove the background with the help of the *Remove background* module included with Microsoft Designer.

The first step is to select the *Edit with AI* tab from the Microsoft Designer home page and select the *Remove background* option. You will see a dialog using which you can either upload or drag/drop the relevant image. The Designer app will ask you to confirm the image. You have to select the *Upload* button as shown in Figure 9-38.

1 file selected from device

Ready to upload this file?

Figure 9-38. *Confirm file uploading*

The background of the uploaded image will be immediately removed (see Figure 9-39) upon selecting the *Upload* button.

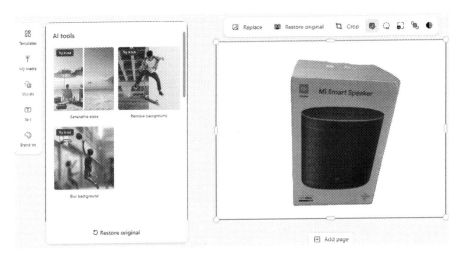

Figure 9-39. *Instantly remove background*

If you analyze Figure 9-39, you can observe that the background of the original image has been removed completely. You can restore the original image and crop the image in addition to other editing tasks using the options from the top navigation bar. You can also text elements, shapes, icons, and filters to the new image. You can save the image to your PC from the Microsoft Designer editor by selecting the *Download* button.

Working with Generative Erase

Microsoft Designer has added the Generative Erase functionality, using which you can erase select objects from images. You can choose objects that need to be removed easily. Let's check out the working of Generative Erase functionality using an image captured from a moving train by the author.

To work with the Generative Erase functionality, you should select the *Edit with AI* tab from the Microsoft Designer dashboard and select the option captioned *Generative erase*. The Designer app prompts you to upload the image. You will see a confirmation dialog as shown in Figure 9-40.

1 file selected from device

Ready to upload this file?

Figure 9-40. *Confirm your action*

You can observe that the image comprises several trees and has been shot inside the train. Hence, you can see the window bar as well. If you select the *Upload* button, the Microsoft Designer editor (Figure 9-41) will open with the uploaded image along with relevant options.

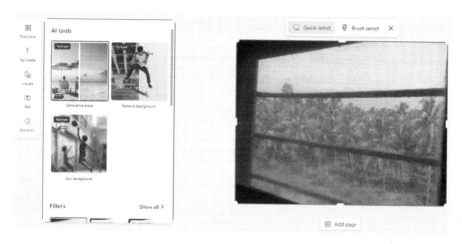

Figure 9-41. *Erase contents quickly via AI*

The next step is to select the *Brush select* option to pick the areas that you need to erase from the original image. You can select the brush size by dragging the slider. A preview of the erase tool will appear immediately upon adjusting the brush size. You can observe from Figure 9-42 that the two window bars have been selected, which will be generatively erased after the competition of this process.

Figure 9-42. *Select the portions that need to be erased*

To erase the objects from the image, you need to select the *Erase object* button. The editor will display a progress indicator while the tool erases the items. The final preview of the image inside the Designer editor after the implementation of Generative Erase looks as shown in Figure 9-43. You can observe that the Generative Erase functionality included with Microsoft Designer works great because it sharply removes the selected objects. You can observe the difference before and after the application of the Generative Erase.

Figure 9-43. *View the AI-erased image*

If you select the *Looks good* button, the Designer editor without the Generative Erase feature will appear on the screen.

Note   Use the Generative Erase feature responsibly.

You can replace the image, remove background, crop, and make use of various Image tools on the top navigation panel. In this way, you can erase properties and items from images as per your requirements.

Restyling Image

Microsoft Designer provides the ability to transform your image with various styles. The output will be a crazy new visual, which you can share on your social media pages to impress your friends. The first step is to select the *Edit with AI* tab and select the *Restyle image* option. You will see a warning message if you work with this module for the first time. The Restyle Image dashboard appears on the screen.

You can upload a photo by selecting the *Image* option. You have to select the *Add image* button and pick your image via any one of the displayed sources as in Figure 9-44.

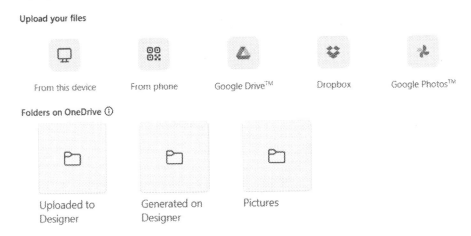

Figure 9-44. *Import images from several sources*

The tool automatically fetches all images from OneDrive and displays them in the menu upon selecting Image. You have to click the *Select* button after uploading an image. The next step is to select a style of your choice as shown in Figure 9-45. Additionally, you can add objects or themes to your image by selecting the *Background elements* option.

Figure 9-45. *Pick a style of your choice*

The final step is to select the *Generate* button. The Restyle Image tool generates four images, and they are displayed under the *My restyled images* tab. You can download and edit by selecting the relevant image. If you select the *Edit* option, the image will appear inside the Designer dashboard.

Note   Microsoft has stated that the restyle feature might not work as expected if there are multiple people in a photo. Please check `https://insider.microsoft365.com/en-us/blog/transform-photos-with-restyle-image-in-microsoft-designer`.

Framing Images

The Frame image module included with Microsoft Designer enables you to enclose images inside beautiful frames. You can decorate your own photo or vacation images depending upon your choice. You should select the *Frame image* option by selecting the *Edit with AI* tab. The Frame image dashboard appears on the screen.

You can add an image, element, and style from the dashboard. Alternatively, you can also manually select a prompt template of your choice from the Frame image dashboard. You will be prompted to upload an image upon selecting a template. Let's upload a scenic image, which we captured during a picnic trip shown in Figure 9-46.

Figure 9-46. *Add an image to create a framed image*

The Elements values are automatically populated along with the relevant selected style. You can modify the style if required at this step. Let's select the *Generate* button to view the framed images in action.

Microsoft Designer generates either three or four images. You can save the image to your PC by clicking the relevant image and selecting the *Download* button. The image can be modified with elements and filters upon selecting the *Edit* button. You can also provide the specific parameters for the frame design like plants, trees, and much more in the prompt. You can report bugs by selecting the *Send feedback* link after opening the image preview. Sometimes, the text will not be added in a frame when you edit via Microsoft Designer. This is the limitation of AI and the corresponding DALL·E model.

Note   The Microsoft Designer user interface changes constantly. You will notice a new Designer home page once in a while. However, the basic working will be the same as discussed in this chapter.

If you had worked with Microsoft Designer before, you would have seen the Brand Kit module. The newly updated Designer app is not included with a brand kit. However, you can edit the existing brand kit via the Designer editor dashboard. You have to select the *Brand kit* icon from the left navigation panel. The Designer displays all the previously created brand kits. You have to point your mouse over the kit and select the *Edit Brand* option. This feature leverages Copilot to create customized brand kits. Microsoft is continuously adding new improvements, and you should check back regularly to observe any change in the brand kit creation process. You can create stunning emojis and clip arts by selecting the relevant option from the Microsoft Designer home page and providing the suitable prompts. Alternatively, you can create images, stickers, avatars, invitations, icons, emojis, clip arts via the Microsoft Designer Android and iOS apps.

Disclaimer   This chapter includes several screenshots of AI-generated images that are captured via Microsoft Designer. The app employs advanced AI and Copilot technologies to generate images. These images have no resemblance to any living persons or characters and are used for the sake of explanation and educational purposes only.

Summary

In this chapter, you've learned the usage of each module included with Microsoft Designer in detail. This chapter examined the process involved in the generation of images, social posts, stickers, invitations, wallpapers, monograms, and much more. You have learned the process involved in the creation of greeting cards. You have also learned about the creation of collages. This feature will be useful if you have multiple images that need to be converted into a single image. You have also learned about the transformation of your image into attractive visuals. You are now in a position to frame images and erase the image objects via AI. The background removal covered in this chapter also plays a key role in your daily life. You will find Microsoft Designer very useful since the app can create attractive visuals that you can showcase on social media platforms. In the next chapter, you will learn the usage of Copilot in Microsoft 365.

CHAPTER 10

Using Copilot in Microsoft 365

Microsoft 365 is a full-blown web-based Office application comprising core apps such as Word, Excel, PowerPoint, OneNote, and Teams. The Copilot support was rolled out to Microsoft 365 apps on March 16, 2023. The purpose of Copilot integration with Microsoft 365 is to simplify the work life, thereby enhancing productivity. Even though Microsoft 365 is oriented for Enterprise users, individuals and their family members can consume Office apps over the cloud with a suitable subscription. You can easily create beautiful articles for your blog and automate the creation of presentations using Copilot. In this chapter, you will learn the usage of Copilot in Microsoft 365 apps.

Getting Started

The first point you need to understand is that you will not be able to leverage the benefits of Copilot immediately after the purchase of a Microsoft 365 subscription. You need a valid license of Microsoft 365 Copilot, which is available as an add-on package if you are an Enterprise user. However, the simplest way to work with Copilot in Microsoft 365 for consumer users is to purchase a Copilot Pro subscription if you have a valid license of Microsoft 365. Sometimes, manufacturers bundle Microsoft

© Anand Narayanaswamy 2024
A. Narayanaswamy, *Microsoft Copilot for Windows 11*, Inside Copilot,
https://doi.org/10.1007/979-8-8688-0583-7_10

365 with their devices. You can check the presence of Microsoft 365 apps on your PC by selecting the *Outlook (new)* icon from the Windows 11 Taskbar. You will see the relevant icons from the navigation panel located on the left side. This is the best way to automate Office apps such as Word, Excel, and PowerPoint. You can opt for a one-month free trial of Copilot Pro to begin with. Let's first examine the steps involved with the purchase of Copilot Pro.

Understanding Copilot Pro

Copilot Free helps you to fetch information and create/rewrite content, including performing basic Windows tasks. You should note that Copilot features are subject to change any notification. The paid version offers all the modules included with the Copilot Free in addition to the ability to create your own GPTs, which is retired by Microsoft in July 2024. However, the paid chatbot delivers responses quickly even during peak times. Copilot Pro also provides support for faster image creation and retails $20 per user/month. You can try Copilot Pro for one month to test-drive the features and functionalities. Copilot Pro is designed to improve not only productivity but also creativity with enhanced image rendering.

Copilot Pro Purchase Process

To work with Copilot Pro, you need to pay for the subscription. The free 30-day trial package enables you to test-drive all the features before arriving at the purchase decision.

The first step is to navigate to www.microsoft.com/en-us/microsoft-copilot and select the *Try Copilot Pro* button located under the Copilot Pro column. You will be prompted to switch over to the Microsoft Store as per your region. For instance, if you are located in India, you should select the *Go to India – English* button. You will now view a new page, www.microsoft.com/en-in/store/b/copilotpro, which provides a detailed overview and tabulated differences between the free and paid versions. You should select the *Start your free trial* button to place an order for the free trial.

Note   The Copilot Pro purchase process mentioned in this section is subject to change as per the discretion of Microsoft.

Alternatively, you can select the *Get Copilot Pro* button (Figure 10-1) from the Copilot dashboard by selecting the *Copilot in Windows (preview)* icon from the Windows 11 Taskbar.

Figure 10-1. Buy Copilot Pro directly from Windows 11

Microsoft Copilot will display the checkout page, as shown in Figure 10-2, from where you can verify and confirm your order. The page specifically mentions about the free trial with a mention that you will be charged $20 every month upon ending of the free trial. Hence, you have to provide the required payment information to work with the trial version.

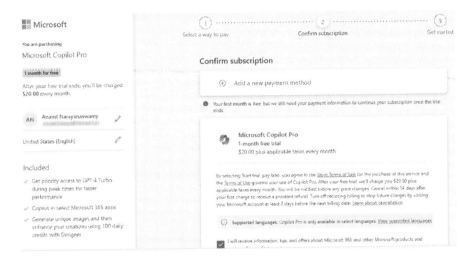

Figure 10-2. *Complete Copilot Pro checkout process*

Note   You can chat with the Microsoft support team from the checkout page in case you encounter an error during the checkout process.

If you are located outside the United States, you have to change your country by selecting the relevant drop-down located on the left side of the checkout page. You need to select the Country (Figure 10-3) from the drop-down and select the *Confirm* button.

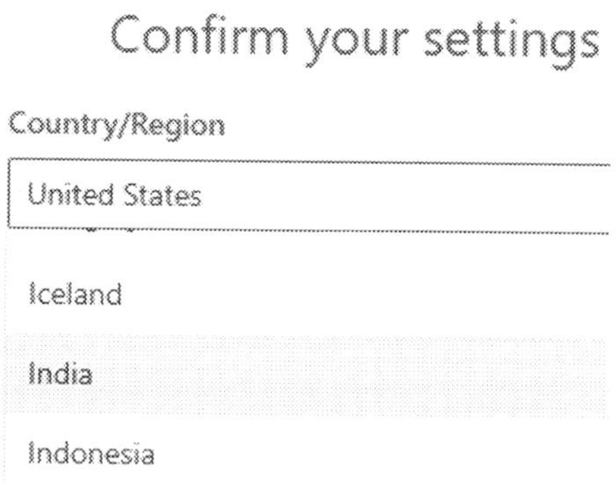

Confirm your settings

Country/Region

United States

Iceland

India

Indonesia

Figure 10-3. *Pick your country before purchase*

The next step involves adding your payment information by clicking the *Next* button. You have to add the required payment information by clicking the Credit card or debit card row. The process involves entering your payment information along with address details. You have to complete the steps outlined in the Copilot dashboard to finalize the purchase. This involves selecting the *Start trial, pay later* button. You will see a confirmation message and email, which will inform you about the next steps.

The Copilot Pro checkout page is designed to automatically charge in recurring mode. However, you can cancel the recurring standing instruction before the first charge. You will receive an email with additional information about Copilot Pro, including the steps required to cancel the subscription. Alternatively, you can install the Microsoft Copilot app from the Google Play Store and Apple App Store to purchase a Copilot Pro subscription.

Working with Copilot in Microsoft 365

To work with Copilot in Microsoft 365, you require access to the *Outlook (new)* app in Windows 11.

> **Tip**   If you are still using the old Mail app in Windows 11, then you can activate the new Outlook app by sliding the *New Outlook* option located on the top-right side.

The Outlook app can be located on the Windows 11 Taskbar in between Microsoft Edge and Microsoft Store icons. The location could change in case you have rearranged or unpinned the icon from the Taskbar. In case you had unpinned the app from the Taskbar, you can use the Windows 11 search to locate the app. You will be able to access the relevant Microsoft 365 apps from the navigation panel on the left side.

> **Note**   If you are unable to view Office app icons inside the Outlook app, then you can navigate to onedrive.com and create the required document or presentation. You should log in to OneDrive using the same Microsoft credentials you used with your Copilot Pro purchase.

Using Copilot in Word

To work with Copilot in Word, you should select the *Outlook (new)* icon from the Windows 11 Taskbar as shown in Figure 10-4.

Figure 10-4. *Start from here*

You will see the Word icon in the navigation panel located on the left side as displayed in Figure 10-5. An alternate way to work with Copilot in Word is to directly navigate to `www.microsoft365.com/launch/word`, from where you can work with Copilot.

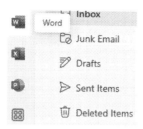

Figure 10-5. *Wordify with Copilot*

The Microsoft 365 dashboard opens upon selecting the Word icon located on the left-side navigation panel. You will see a series of explanatory notes as a welcome message. These notes provide a short introduction about the importance of Copilot in Microsoft 365. You can either create a new document or open an existing Word document. Let's create a new Word document (Figure 10-6) by selecting the *Blank document* icon.

Figure 10-6. *Start automating Word*

To work with Copilot, you should click the gray-colored Copilot icon as shown in Figure 10-7.

Select the icon or press Alt + i to draft with Copilot

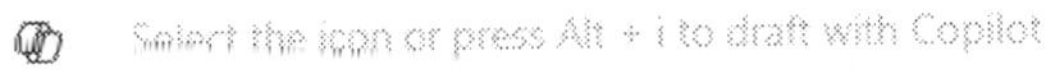

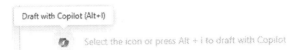

Figure 10-7. *Start your Copilot journey*

You will be able to view the colored Copilot icon (Figure 10-8) if you point your mouse over the icon.

Draft with Copilot (Alt+I)
Select the icon or press Alt + i to draft with Copilot

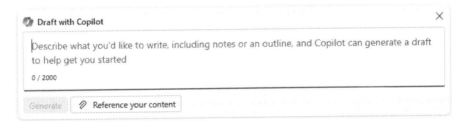

Figure 10-8. *Copilot kick-start signal*

Alternatively, you can also make use of the *Alt+i* keyboard shortcut to work with Copilot. If you select the Copilot icon, you will see a prompt dialog box as shown in Figure 10-9.

Draft with Copilot
Describe what you'd like to write, including notes or an outline, and Copilot can generate a draft to help get you started
0 / 2000
Generate
Reference your content

Figure 10-9. *Prompt Word*

You have to provide a suitable prompt, which can be up to 2000 words as displayed in Figure 10-10.

Figure 10-10. *Ask Copilot to do this with Word*

The prompt is about the creation of an article related to AI with advantages, disadvantages, and conclusion. Copilot shows the progress as shown in Figure 10-11.

Figure 10-11. *Wait until Copilot generates content*

In Figure 10-12, you can view how nicely Copilot generates and displays the article with the required length for improved SEO. You can also ask Copilot to generate long articles if required.

Figure 10-12. *Read the Copilot-generated article*

Copilot not only generates the article but also the editor score (Figure 10-13), which is 89% for our article. The spelling and grammar should be resolved to make the score 100%.

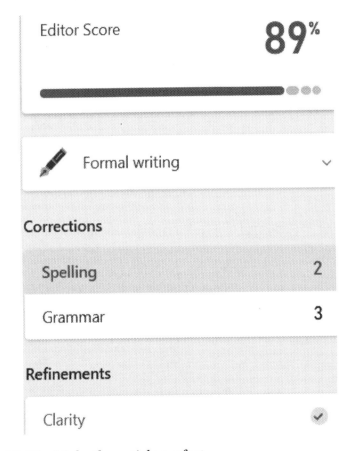

Figure 10-13. *Make the article perfect*

The entire process is automated. If you select the *Spelling* option from the editor, Copilot takes you to the relevant location inside the content with spelling suggestions as shown in Figure 10-14.

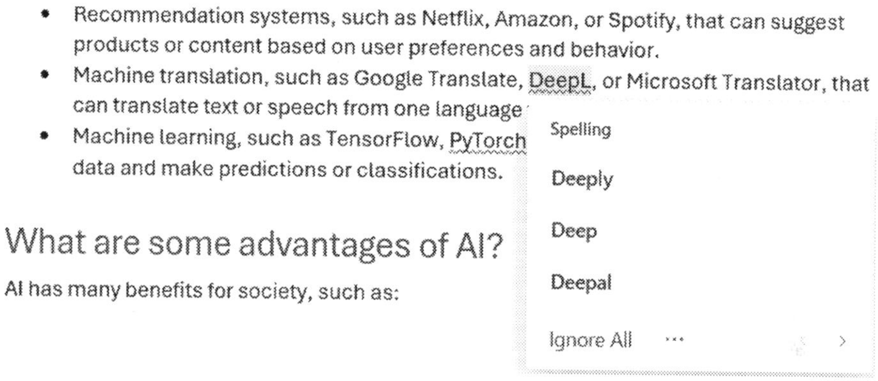

- Recommendation systems, such as Netflix, Amazon, or Spotify, that can suggest products or content based on user preferences and behavior.
- Machine translation, such as Google Translate, DeepL, or Microsoft Translator, that can translate text or speech from one language
- Machine learning, such as TensorFlow, PyTorch, data and make predictions or classifications.

Spelling

Deeply

What are some advantages of AI?

Deep

AI has many benefits for society, such as:

Deepal

Ignore All   ⋯   >

Figure 10-14. *Rectify mistakes on the go*

If you select *Grammar*, Copilot points out the relevant word that requires correction as displayed in Figure 10-15. You should note that these features are part of an advanced editor, which will be available only for seven days from the date of editor upgradation.

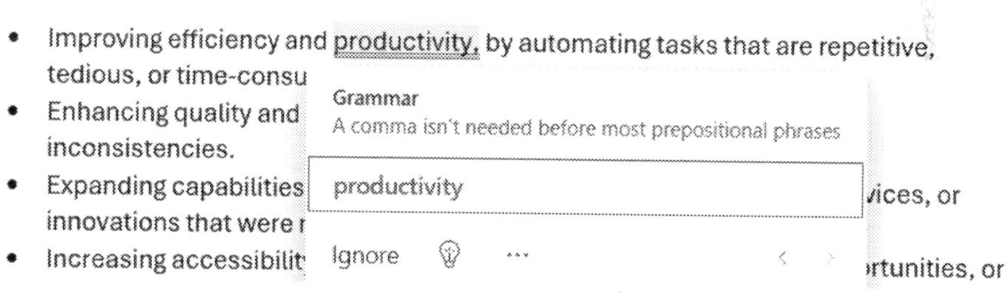

- Improving efficiency and productivity, by automating tasks that are repetitive, tedious, or time-consu
- Enhancing quality and inconsistencies.
- Expanding capabilities innovations that were r
- Increasing accessibilit

Grammar
A comma isn't needed before most prepositional phrases

productivity

ices, or

Ignore   💡   ⋯   < >   rtunities, or

Figure 10-15. *Don't worry about English grammar*

Copilot in Word is also capable of generating content in tabular format as shown in Figure 10-16.

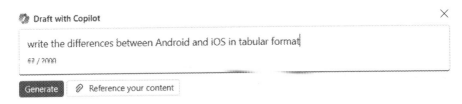

Figure 10-16. *Asking Copilot to generate tabular content*

In Figure 10-17, you can clearly visualize how Copilot displays the relevant information in tabular format.

Android	iOS
An operating system developed by Google, based on the Linux kernel and designed for touchscreen devices.	An operating system developed by Apple, based on the Darwin kernel and designed for iPhone, iPad, and iPod Touch.
Open source, meaning anyone can modify or customize the code and use it for their own devices or applications.	Closed source, meaning only Apple can access and modify the code and use it for their own devices or applications.
Has a larger market share and more device diversity, with many manufacturers producing different models and specifications.	Has a smaller market share and less device diversity, with only Apple producing a limited number of models and specifications.
Offers more flexibility and customization, allowing users to change the appearance, functionality, and settings of their devices and applications.	Offers less flexibility and customization, requiring users to follow the predefined appearance, functionality, and settings of their devices and applications.
Has a higher risk of malware and security breaches, due to the lack of standardization and regulation of the software and hardware.	Has a lower risk of malware and security breaches, due to the strict control and supervision of the software and hardware.
Has a wider range of app availability and compatibility, with more apps being developed and supported for the platform.	Has a narrower range of app availability and compatibility, with some apps being exclusive or optimized for the platform.
Has a lower cost and quality, with cheaper and more affordable devices and applications, but also lower performance and durability.	Has a higher cost and quality, with more expensive and premium devices and applications, but also higher performance and durability.

Figure 10-17. *Copilot simplifies complex content creation*

You should also note that Copilot in Word automatically summarizes content by drilling down large files. Let's load a preloaded content and try to summarize the content. The first step after loading the file is to select the Copilot icon from the Word Toolbar. You will see the Copilot interface as shown in Figure 10-18.

Understand
Summarize this doc [in 3 key points]
Ask
How can I more concisely describe [time management?]

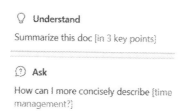

Figure 10-18. *Easily summarize a document*

The prompt is to summarize the content in Chapter 11, which has been loaded and active on the Word editor. You should note that Copilot in Word displays several progress indicators before finally dropping the summarized content as shown in Figure 10-19.

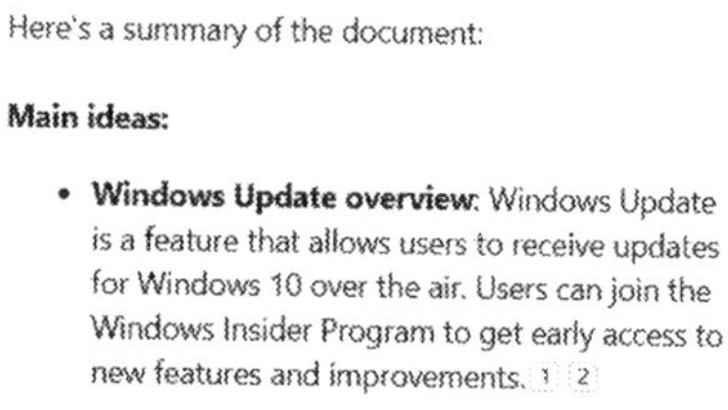

Here's a summary of the document:
Main ideas:
Windows Update overview: Windows Update is a feature that allows users to receive updates for Windows 10 over the air. Users can join the Windows Insider Program to get early access to new features and improvements.
1
2

Figure 10-19. *View the summarized content*

Copilot also displays automated suggestions below the generated content, which you can make use of if required. It's so easy not only to create quality content in any format but also summarize an existing document with Copilot in Word. You can try by loading different content-loaded Word files.

Note   Microsoft provides access to a premium editor for free with advanced writing assistance. You can try the editor for seven days and then upgrade to Microsoft 365 for Copilot for unlimited premium suggestions.

Using Copilot in Excel

Microsoft Excel is a popular spreadsheet application used by several business and corporate entities, including individuals. Copilot in Excel automates the work involved with the spreadsheet quickly. You can easily create charts, PivotCharts, and PivotTables using Copilot. However, there are basic requirements that you need to follow before starting to work with Copilot in Excel. The required data for Copilot analysis should be provided as an Excel table. You can add data to the workbook, but you should format it as a table. The data should also be on a supported range. Moreover, the relevant Excel workbook should be on OneDrive or SharePoint.

To work with Copilot in Excel, you should first select the *Excel* icon from the navigation pane located on the left side using the Outlook app. Alternatively, you can also select the *Excel* icon from within the Microsoft 365 app. The first step is to create a blank workbook as shown in Figure 10-20.

Figure 10-20. *Start Copiloting from here*

The Copilot icon is located on the Toolbar as shown in Figure 10-21. You can notice the difference in the icon color.

Figure 10-21. *Hit the Copilot icon when ready*

Let's open a template included in Excel for the purpose of our discussion (Figure 10-22) and ask Copilot to calculate the total actual work. As you can observe, Copilot displays the result on the dashboard.

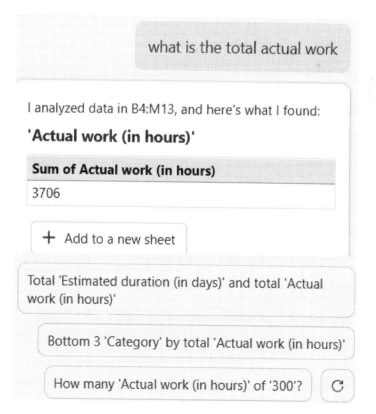

Figure 10-22. *Ask Copilot with questions*

You can also ask Copilot to summarize the document. You can observe that Copilot in Excel clearly displays the summary in graphical format together with a crisp explanation as displayed in Figure 10-23. You can also copy the generated summarized copy and use it elsewhere.

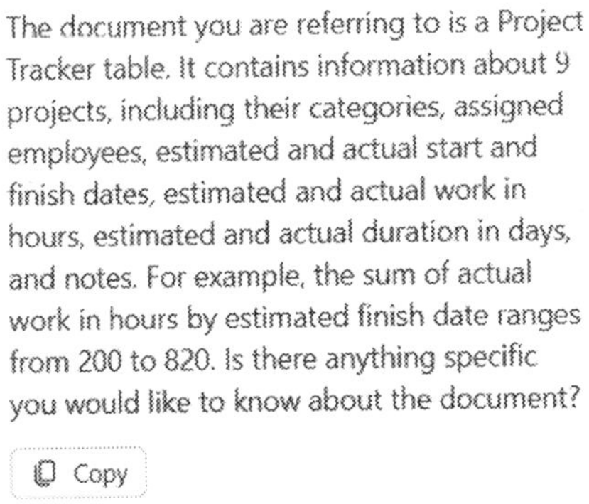

The document you are referring to is a Project Tracker table. It contains information about 9 projects, including their categories, assigned employees, estimated and actual start and finish dates, estimated and actual work in hours, estimated and actual duration in days, and notes. For example, the sum of actual work in hours by estimated finish date ranges from 200 to 820. Is there anything specific you would like to know about the document?

 Copy

Figure 10-23. *Summarize the Excel workbook with Copilot*

Copilot in Excel will be useful for those involved in the accounting profession since they can easily evaluate the Excel workbook quickly. You can also add formula columns, highlight, sort, and filter the relevant Excel workbook. Microsoft recommends that the query you provide in Copilot should be descriptive for efficient results.

Note   Create a blank workbook by opening the Excel app within Microsoft 365. You should add Name, Marks as column names. The next step is to add and select the required data. Select Insert ➤ Table and choose OK from the displayed dialog. Switch back to the Home tab and select the Copilot icon. Provide a prompt like *How many marks did Arun scored* and observe the output.

Copilot in PowerPoint

Microsoft PowerPoint is a powerful presentation tool using which you can create stunning presentations. In addition to slides, you can add images, videos, and much more to amplify your content. Copilot is designed with an ability to automate all complex tasks associated with the creation of a presentation. You just need to provide a suitable topic, and Copilot will create all the required content with stock images.

To work with Copilot in PowerPoint, you should select the *PowerPoint* icon from the left-side navigation panel of either the new Outlook app or Microsoft 365. Let's get started by creating an empty presentation by selecting the *Blank presentation* option. You will see a screen as shown in Figure 10-24.

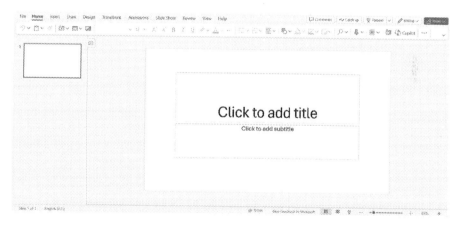

Figure 10-24. *Kick-start your Copilot journey with PowerPoint*

The next step is to select the Copilot icon from the top Toolbar. You will see a user interface as shown in Figure 10-25.

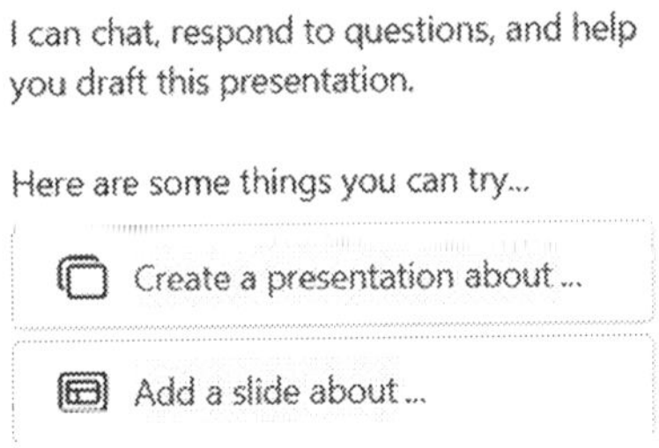

I can chat, respond to questions, and help
you draft this presentation.

Here are some things you can try...

    ▢ Create a presentation about ...

    ▣ Add a slide about ...

Figure 10-25. *Decide what to do with Copilot*

You can now ask Copilot to create a new PowerPoint presentation by
providing a suitable prompt. If you select the first option from Figure 10-25,
Copilot displays a prompt window (Figure 10-26) with relevant default
content. You just need to provide the topic for which you need a
presentation.

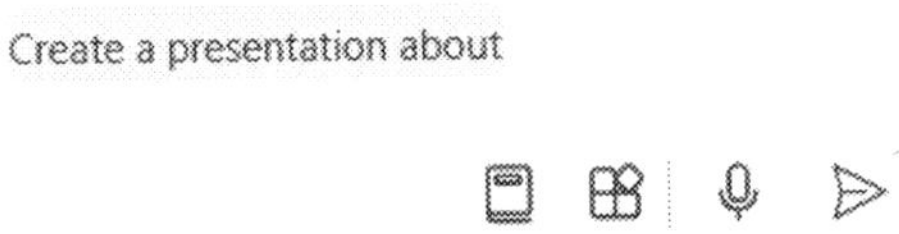

Create a presentation about

▢ ▣ 🎤 ▷

Figure 10-26. *Supply your prompt here*

Let's ask Copilot to create a PowerPoint presentation about the
evolution of computers. A confirmation message will be displayed when
Copilot completes the creation of the presentation. As you can observe
from Figure 10-27, Copilot intelligently creates slides with relevant content
and images.

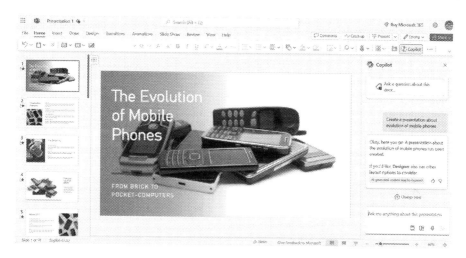

Figure 10-27. *Copilot creates a stunning automated presentation*

You can also ask a question about the active presentation by selecting the relevant option from the right-side navigation. The *Ask a question about this deck* option appears only after the creation of the slide. You can add additional slides by providing a specific prompt. Copilot provides endless possibilities in your quest to create stunning presentations.

Create Presentation from File

With Copilot in PowerPoint, you can easily create presentations from a Word file. You just need to point out the location of the Word file, and Copilot will complete the complex task associated with the creation of the presentation. The main point to note is that you should create a link to the Word file on OneDrive to instruct Copilot to create a presentation. You can use Word files directly from Copilot in Excel only if you have a Microsoft 365 Copilot subscription on top of a Microsoft 365 paid license.

Note   Copilot in PowerPoint creates presentations from files that are available inside your OneDrive Personal workspace.

For the purpose of this chapter, we've used a Word file that's available inside OneDrive. You can reference the Word file in Copilot by creating a shareable link from OneDrive. This can be done by navigating to OneDrive – Personal and locating the Word file. You should then right-click the file name and select the *Share* option from the pop-up menu as shown in Figure 10-28.

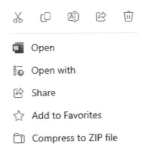

Figure 10-28. *Sharing the OneDrive file*

The next step is to select the *Copy* button from the *Copy link* section as displayed in Figure 10-29.

Figure 10-29. *Grab the OneDrive file link*

You will see a new dialog with the relevant link to the Word file. You should copy the link and create a blank PowerPoint presentation using Microsoft 365. The next step is to provide a prompt to enable Copilot to create a PowerPoint file from the Word file. If you don't know the prompt, you can easily find it out by clicking the *View prompts* (Figure 10-30) icon from the *Prompt* textbox.

Figure 10-30. *View automated prompts*

You will see options to create, edit, and ask Copilot as shown in Figure 10-31.

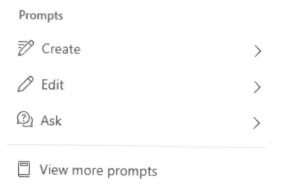

Figure 10-31. *Decide the work with Copilot*

In Figure 10-32, you can see several prompts that are automatically displayed upon selecting the *Create* option.

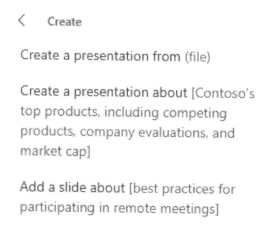

Figure 10-32. *Pick an action of your choice*

If you select the first prompt, then it will be automatically placed inside the textbox as displayed in Figure 10-33.

Figure 10-33. Type your context here

You can now paste the OneDrive share link, and the PowerPoint presentation will be created upon selecting the *Send* button. Copilot in PowerPoint displays the generated presentation (Figure 10-34), which you can modify depending on your requirements. You can change fonts, add images, and much more. As you can observe, Copilot has created 25 slides with the content scraped from our Word file.

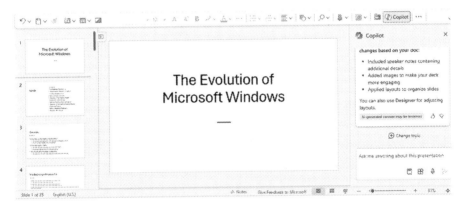

Figure 10-34. View the generated PowerPoint presentation

The time required to create the presentation depends upon the length of the content in the Word file. You will see a progress bar as shown in Figure 10-35.

Generating slides (24%)...

⊗ Stop generating

Figure 10-35. *Copilot displays progress*

Using Automated Prompts

You can view additional prompts by selecting the *View more prompts* option in Figure 10-31. Copilot in PowerPoint displays the available prompts from Copilot Lab as shown in Figure 10-36.

Prompts from Copilot Lab

🔖 Saved prompts

| Task ∨ | Job type ∨ |

✏️ **Add an image**
Add an image of [a puppy dog]

📝 **Create a vacation presentation**
Create a presentation about [Hawaii]

Figure 10-36. *Work intelligently with Copilot*

The prompts are related to PowerPoint, and you simply need to fill up the blanks to enable Copilot to create content. You will find these automated prompt ideas useful if you don't have any idea about the usage of Copilot in PowerPoint.

Microsoft Copilot is available with commercial data protection to the Microsoft 365 mobile app for Android and iOS platforms. This includes Microsoft 365 integration in Word and PowerPoint mobile. You can now directly compose content and create presentations via Copilot using your Android device.

You can ask Copilot to create a new presentation or slide or organize/summarize an existing presentation. Do you want to know the key slides in a presentation? You just need to open the relevant presentation and select the *Show key slides* prompt. Let's try to create a presentation about an activity. You can't edit the automated prompts but can provide a suitable context. The resulting output looks as displayed in Figure 10-37.

Figure 10-37. *Create presentations in a flash*

The presentation is not lengthy but provides all the essential facts along with images. You can convert PowerPoint presentations into videos with the help of third-party software tools like Veed. You can experiment with all the prompts included with Copilot Lab to know the functionality.

Copilot in Outlook

Microsoft Outlook is a popular email client tool using which you send and receive emails. With Copilot in Outlook, you can compose email messages easily. You just need to provide a prompt or context, and the Copilot will do the rest of the work.

To work with Copilot in Outlook, open the Outlook (new) app via the Windows 11 Taskbar and select the *New mail* button (Figure 10-38), which is located at the top-left side.

Figure 10-38. *Create a new email*

You can compose an email by providing the required parameters such as the recipient email address, subject, and the message. Let's generate content via Copilot by selecting its icon from the top right-side Toolbar as shown in Figure 10-39.

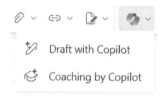

Figure 10-39. *Copilot modules in Outlook*

You should select the *Draft with Copilot* option and provide the relevant prompt or context (Figure 10-40) for which the email message should be generated.

Figure 10-40. *Prompting Outlook*

Copilot in Outlook generates the required content (Figure 10-41) as per the provided prompt.

Figure 10-41. Quickly generate email content with Copilot

The query was to ask Anand to complete the Copilot book project by Wednesday. As you can see, Copilot in Outlook generates the required message. You can either retain the output generated by Copilot or discard it and start over. If you select the *Keep it* button, then the message will be added to the *Compose* editor.

Copilot in Outlook also enables you to modify the generated content automatically by selecting the *Edit Prompt* icon located above the *Keep it* icon. The list of options will be displayed as shown in Figure 10-42.

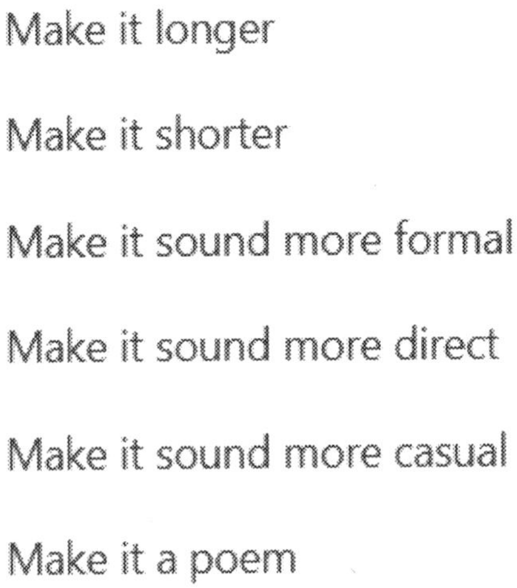

Make it longer

Make it shorter

Make it sound more formal

Make it sound more direct

Make it sound more casual

Make it a poem

Figure 10-42. Change the generated content

You also provide a short prompt for coaching purposes and ask Copilot to draft a message as displayed in Figure 10-43. The sample prompt should be at least 100 characters in length and include the relevant context.

Request Mark to arrive for meeting 30 minutes in advance for a PowerPoint presentation

Figure 10-43. *Coach yourself Copilot*

You should then select the *Try Draft with Copilot* button, which will add the context to the *Draft with Copilot* prompt box. Copilot in Outlook generates a message upon selecting the *Generate* button as shown in Figure 10-44.

Figure 10-44. *Copilot generates perfect content*

Modifying Content Style Using Email Coaching

You can change the tone and length of the content that needs to be generated by selecting the *Generation Options* icon. You will see a list of options as shown in Figure 10-45.

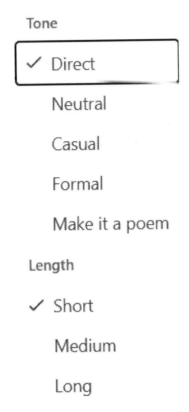

Figure 10-45. Modify the content style

A tick mark will be visible against the tone and length. You can use the context and ask Copilot to generate the required content. You can easily make use of Copilot not only to simplify your daily messaging tasks but also to enhance productivity. Microsoft recently released Copilot Use Cases eBook with information about real-world implementations. You can download the book by navigating to `https://info.microsoft.com/ww-landing-inspired-by-ai-six-copilot-use-cases.html`.

Summary

Copilot in Microsoft 365 helps you to simplify tasks associated with your favorite apps such as Word, Excel, and PowerPoint. The integration of Copilot in Word helps you to create content easily. You can even ask Copilot to summarize and fetch information from an existing document. It's now easy to automate Excel workbooks with the help of Copilot. You also learned the steps required to create a PowerPoint presentation via Copilot. You just need to provide the required prompt to create content and powerful presentations that can be converted into blog posts and videos. You also learned how easy it is to compose email messages with the help of Copilot integration in Outlook. Moreover, the integration of Copilot in Word and PowerPoint mobile is a step in the right direction. In the next chapter, you will learn the usage of Microsoft Copilot with the Windows app.

CHAPTER 11

Learning Microsoft Copilot with Windows App

In the previous chapters, you learned about the usage of Microsoft Copilot without installing any external apps. You learned about accessing Copilot via Windows 11, Microsoft Edge, Bing, and Skype. Windows 11 ships with Copilot in select regions and can be accessed from the Taskbar by selecting the Copilot in Windows (preview) icon. Microsoft Copilot is now available as a stand-alone app and can be installed via the Microsoft Store. You can perform all the actions associated with Copilot using the Windows app. In this chapter, you will learn the usage of Microsoft Copilot with the help of the recently launched Windows app.

Getting Started

Microsoft Copilot is available as a stand-alone Windows app, which can be used just like any other app like Notepad and Paint. The first step is to navigate to the Microsoft Store by selecting the Windows 11 Taskbar icon as displayed in Figure 11-1. You should note that the Windows app is just a wrapper of https://copilot.microsoft.com. This means the app inherits all the features that are available when you access the web dashboard.

© Anand Narayanaswamy 2024
A. Narayanaswamy, *Microsoft Copilot for Windows 11*, Inside Copilot,
https://doi.org/10.1007/979-8-8688-0583-7_11

Figure 11-1. Opening the Microsoft Store

Note   You can also manually download the installer and complete the Copilot app installation process: `https://apps.microsoft.com/detail/9nht9rb2f4hd?hl=en-us&gl=US`.

The Microsoft Store dashboard will display on the screen. You have to locate the Microsoft Copilot app from the top search bar. The app will be visible on the dashboard as shown in Figure 11-2.

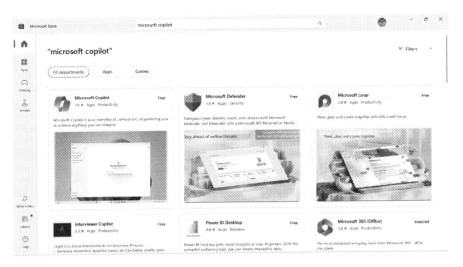

Figure 11-2. Navigate the Microsoft Store

In Figure 11-3, you can view the Microsoft Copilot app page inside the store. You can scroll down to read reviews, features, system requirements, and other parameters related to the app.

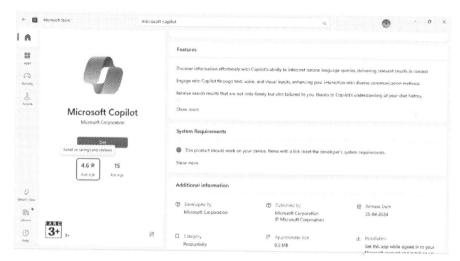

Figure 11-3. *Proceeding to install Copilot*

The next step is to select the *Get* button to install the app. The time required to install the app depends upon the system configuration and speed of your Internet connectivity.

Note   The advantage of the Microsoft Copilot Windows app is that you can open and work either by selecting the Taskbar or by double-clicking the desktop icon. You can also open the Copilot app using the Windows 11 search box. You now have a choice of several options instead of solely depending upon the Copilot in Windows (preview) icon near the Notifications icon on the Taskbar.

The relevant notification will display in Windows 11 after the successful installation of the app. Moreover, the *Get* button caption will change itself to *Open*, where when clicked the Microsoft Copilot Windows app dashboard will appear on the screen as shown in Figure 11-4.

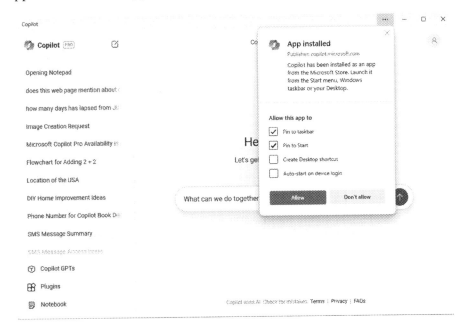

Figure 11-4. *Decide where to keep the Copilot Windows app*

You have the choice to place the Copilot app on the Taskbar, Start menu or Desktop. Additionally, you can set the app to start automatically when the system boots.

Tip   You can work with Microsoft Copilot using Android and iOS devices by downloading the app from the Google Play Store and Apple App Store, respectively.

Windows 11 will prompt you to confirm whether the Copilot app should be pinned on the Taskbar. The dashboard of the Copilot Windows app looks as shown in Figure 11-5.

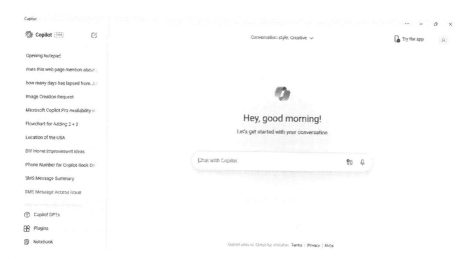

Figure 11-5. *Copilot Windows app dashboard*

Prompting the Windows App

You can provide the prompt as text, upload an image, or use voice to dictate the query. You can also upload PDF files as prompt, but you need a Microsoft 365 Business license. As of this writing, the PDF functionality is not available for consumers with Copilot Free and even with a Pro subscription. You have to select a suitable conversation style by selecting the drop-down located at the top of the app dashboard as shown in Figure 11-6. The default style is Creative, but you can change to Balanced or Precise according to your preference.

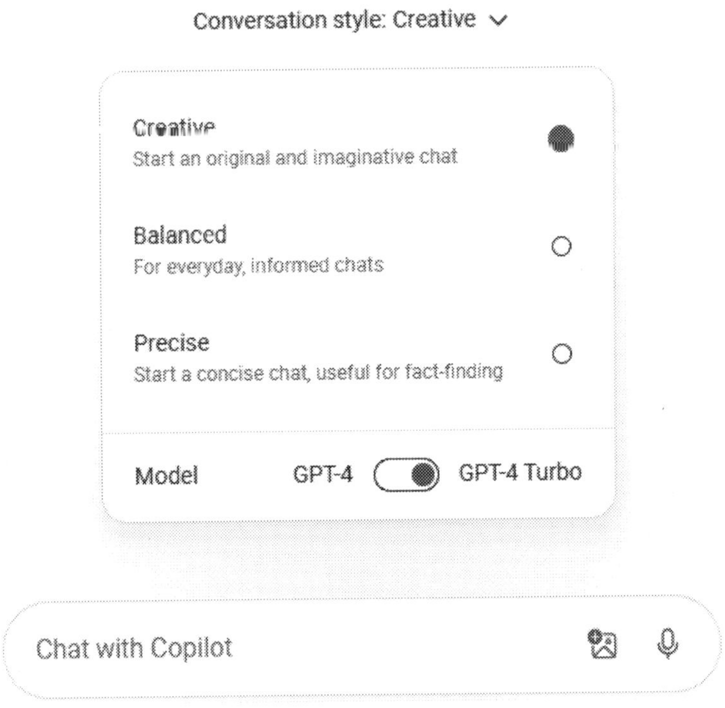

Conversation style: Creative ∨

Creative
Start an original and imaginative chat ●

Balanced
For everyday, informed chats ○

Precise
Start a concise chat, useful for fact-finding ○

Model   GPT-4 (●) GPT-4 Turbo

Chat with Copilot

Figure 11-6. *Select your output tone*

Caution   Microsoft is currently experimenting with a new version
of Copilot without any conversation style options. However, the styles
could appear for free users randomly based on the region. Please
note that the conversation styles might appear only for Copilot Pro
subscribers. You can manually activate the conversation styles even
if you don't have Copilot Pro subscription. You should select the
Profile icon from the top right side, choose *Settings* and modify the
Country/Region to *United States - English*. Whatever may be the
scenario, the functionality of Copilot remains the same.

The default model is marked as GPT-4 Turbo because of the active Copilot Pro subscription. The system generates high-quality content because of the addition of the latest GPT model. You can also access Copilot GPTs, plugins, and Notebook from the navigation panel on the left side.

Let's test the working of the Copilot Windows app by providing a simple prompt (Figure 11-7) inside the *Chat with Copilot* textbox. The text area will automatically expand as you type the prompt.

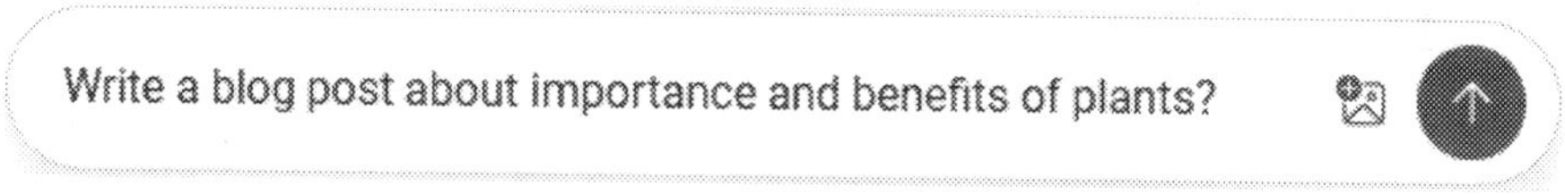

Write a blog post about importance and benefits of plants?

Figure 11-7. *View the Copilot Windows app response*

In Figure 11-8, you can view the response that is displayed inside the Copilot Windows app. You can also scroll down and view additional content. The Copilot app also fetches the conversation history from your interactions with the web-based interface and is displayed on the left side.

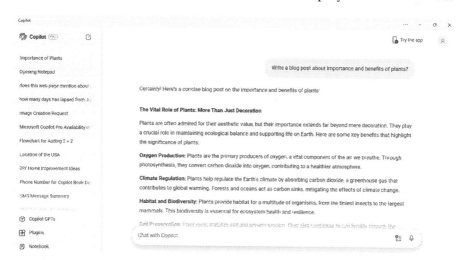

Figure 11-8. *View the response generated by Copilot Windows app*

You can copy and share the content if you point your mouse over the response generated by the Copilot Windows app. Moreover, you can also hear the response by selecting *Read aloud* option. You will be able to like, dislike and export the content by selecting the three vertical dots. You can create a new request by selecting the icon from the top-left side as shown in Figure 11-9.

Figure 11-9. *Ask Copilot another query*

Let's try another example (Figure 11-10) by asking Copilot to generate a list of top five Windows 11 laptops in tabular format.

List top five Windows 11 laptops with all the important features in tabular format

Figure 11-10. *Can Copilot generate responses in tables?*

You can observe from Figure 11-11 how nicely Copilot tabulates relevant information and generates the output inside the dashboard.

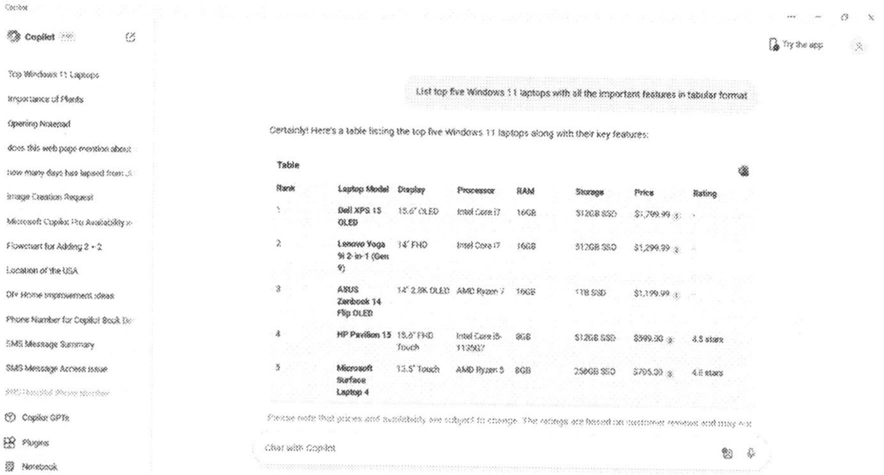

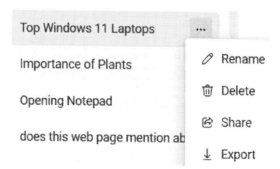

Figure 11-11. *View the Copilot-generated tabulated content*

You can share and export the Copilot response by pointing your mouse over the prompt name on the conversation history from the navigation panel on the left side. You will see three horizontal dots on the right side, which you should select to view the relevant options as shown in Figure 11-12.

Figure 11-12. *Showcase the Copilot results*

You can share the results on social media platforms like Facebook, X, Pinterest, LinkedIn, Reddit, and OneNote. You can also copy the link or share via email from the dialog displayed in Figure 11-13.

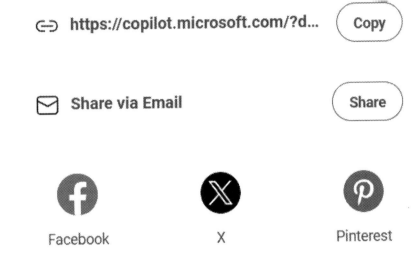

Figure 11-13. *Publish the Copilot work on social media*

The Copilot app also enables you to export the generated response in Word, PDF, and text formats by selecting the *Export* option from the displayed menu as shown in Figure 11-14.

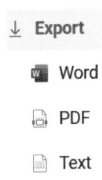

Figure 11-14. *Save content instantly*

Working with Copilot GPTs

You can also create and work with Copilot GPTs with the help of the Windows app as shown in Figure 11-15.

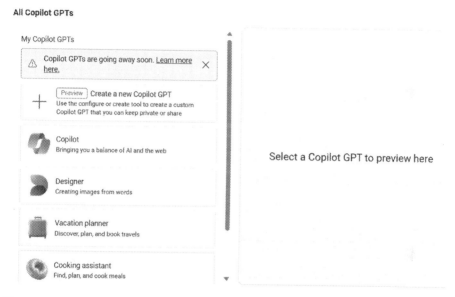

Figure 11-15. *Easily work with Copilot GPTs*

The Copilot Pro subscription enables users to create their own Copilot GPTs in addition to the GPTs offered by Microsoft. With the help of default GPTs, users were able to create AI images easily as well as plan vacations properly. The fitness GPT helped users to keep track of their health.

Note   Microsoft discontinued the usage of the Copilot GPT functionality as well as the ability to create customized GPTs in July 2024. This feature is currently available only for Commercial and Enterprise customers. Copilot GPTs created by Microsoft and those created by customers have been completely removed.

For instance, if you select Designer Copilot GPT and click the *Get started* button, the user interface will change, and the designer module will be activated as shown in Figure 11-16.

Figure 11-16. *Designer GPT in action*

You can then ask Copilot to generate images by providing the relevant prompt such as *A lone astronaut floating in a sea of stars, holding a single glowing flower.* The Copilot app displays the generated images.

Creating Your Own GPTs

You now know that the Copilot Pro subscription will help you to create your own GPTs. Let's examine the steps required to create them. Firstly, you should open the Copilot Windows app and select the Copilot GPTs option. You will see all the GPTs in the corresponding dialog as shown in Figure 11-17.

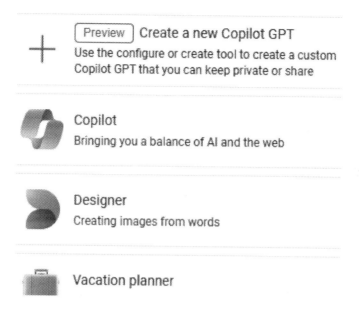

Figure 11-17. *Custom GPT creation starts here*

The next step is to select the *Create a new Copilot GPT* option. In Figure 11-18, you can view the Copilot GPT Settings dashboard which will display upon selecting the option.

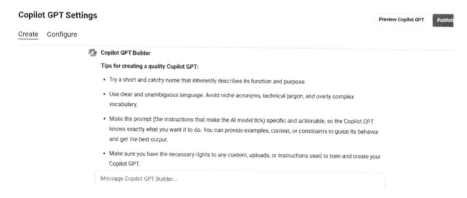

Figure 11-18. *Provide a context for custom GPT*

You can make use of the Copilot GPT Builder to provide suitable data based on which Copilot creates the GPT. You can read the tips to get started. You can also manually provide (Figure 11-19) the name, description, instructions, and other data by selecting the *Configure* tab.

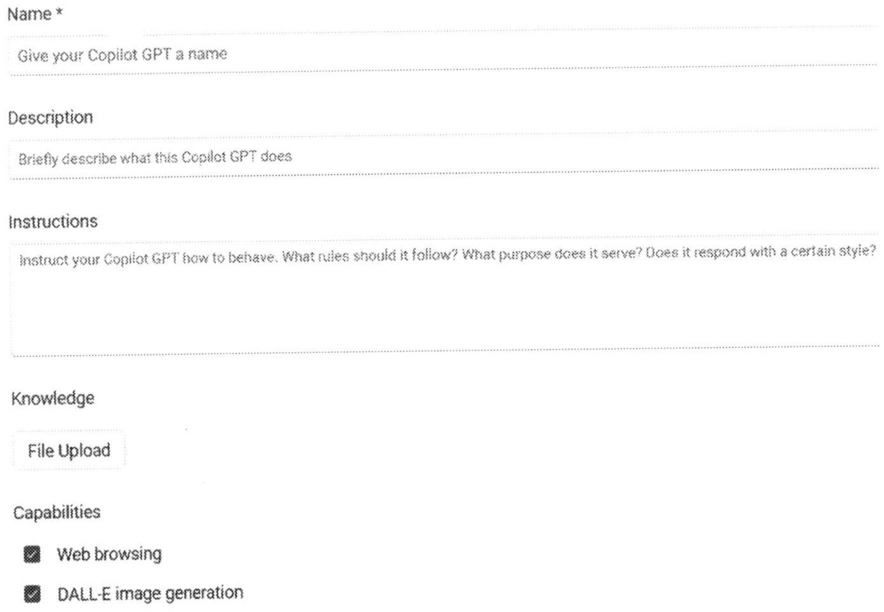

Name *

Give your Copilot GPT a name

Description

Briefly describe what this Copilot GPT does

Instructions

Instruct your Copilot GPT how to behave. What rules should it follow? What purpose does it serve? Does it respond with a certain style?

Knowledge

File Upload

Capabilities

- Web browsing
- DALL-E image generation

Figure 11-19. Manually provide data for custom GPTs

The best way is to use the builder and follow the instructions displayed on the screen. Copilot will ask you a question as you provide each data. Let's get started by providing the prompt *learning JavaScript*. Figure 11-20 shows the response based on our context. Copilot will now ask you to confirm a name for your GPT by providing an intelligent suggestion.

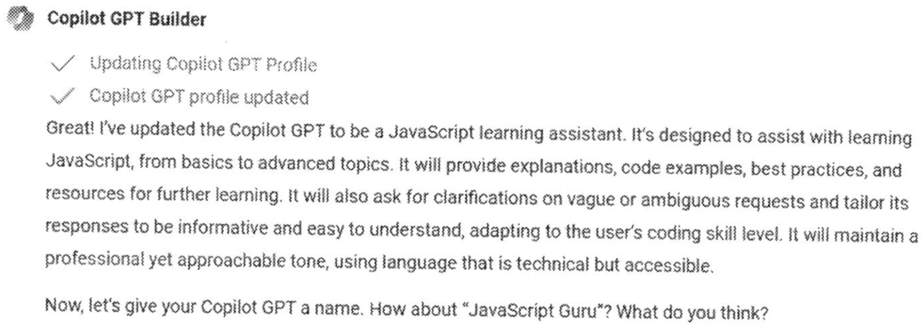

Copilot GPT Builder

✓ Updating Copilot GPT Profile

✓ Copilot GPT profile updated

Great! I've updated the Copilot GPT to be a JavaScript learning assistant. It's designed to assist with learning JavaScript, from basics to advanced topics. It will provide explanations, code examples, best practices, and resources for further learning. It will also ask for clarifications on vague or ambiguous requests and tailor its responses to be informative and easy to understand, adapting to the user's coding skill level. It will maintain a professional yet approachable tone, using language that is technical but accessible.

Now, let's give your Copilot GPT a name. How about "JavaScript Guru"? What do you think?

Figure 11-20. *Confirm your custom GPT name here*

As you can see, Copilot displays a confirmation message (Figure 11-21) upon accepting the automated Copilot GPT name. You can further refine the system by providing additional data if available.

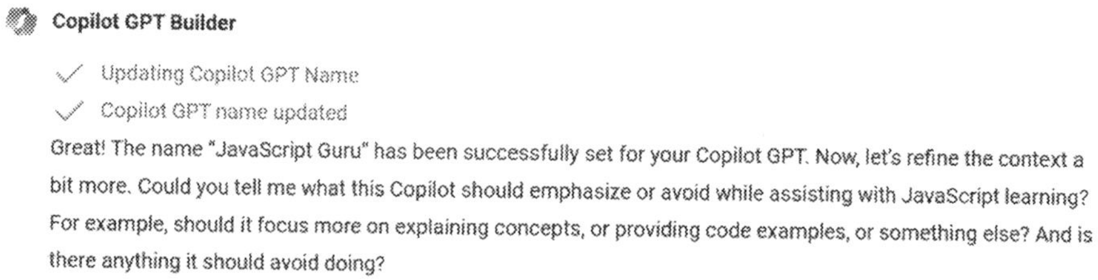

Copilot GPT Builder

✓ Updating Copilot GPT Name

✓ Copilot GPT name updated

Great! The name "JavaScript Guru" has been successfully set for your Copilot GPT. Now, let's refine the context a bit more. Could you tell me what this Copilot should emphasize or avoid while assisting with JavaScript learning? For example, should it focus more on explaining concepts, or providing code examples, or something else? And is there anything it should avoid doing?

Figure 11-21. *Copilot GPT created*

Copilot GPT can be accessed by selecting the *Preview Copilot GPT* button located on the top-right side. Figure 11-22 displays the custom Copilot dashboard that we created.

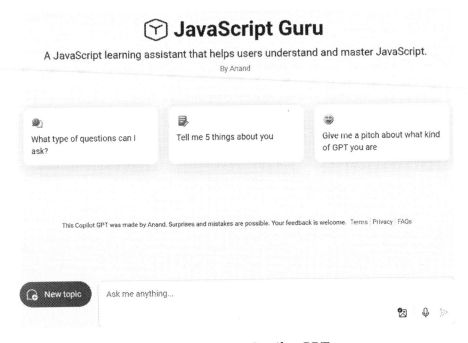

Figure 11-22. Experience your own Copilot GPT

You should provide the required prompt as you normally do with Copilot. In this way, you can experiment with the creation of custom GPTs.

Using Copilot Plugins

The Copilot app enables you to work with plugins. The list of plugins will display as shown in Figure 11-23 upon selecting the Plugins option. You should note that the list of available plugins varies by country and region. Microsoft Copilot is under continuous development, and hence you can expect new plugins over the upcoming months.

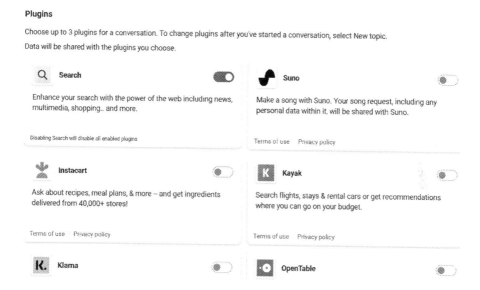

Plugins

Choose up to 3 plugins for a conversation. To change plugins after you've started a conversation, select New topic.

Data will be shared with the plugins you choose.

Figure 11-23. *Activate and work with Copilot plugins*

Let's enable the Suno plugin and ask Copilot to generate a melody song. The system automatically generates the song and displays it inside the dashboard as shown in Figure 11-24. You can then download or share the generated song as well as listen to it directly from the Copilot dashboard.

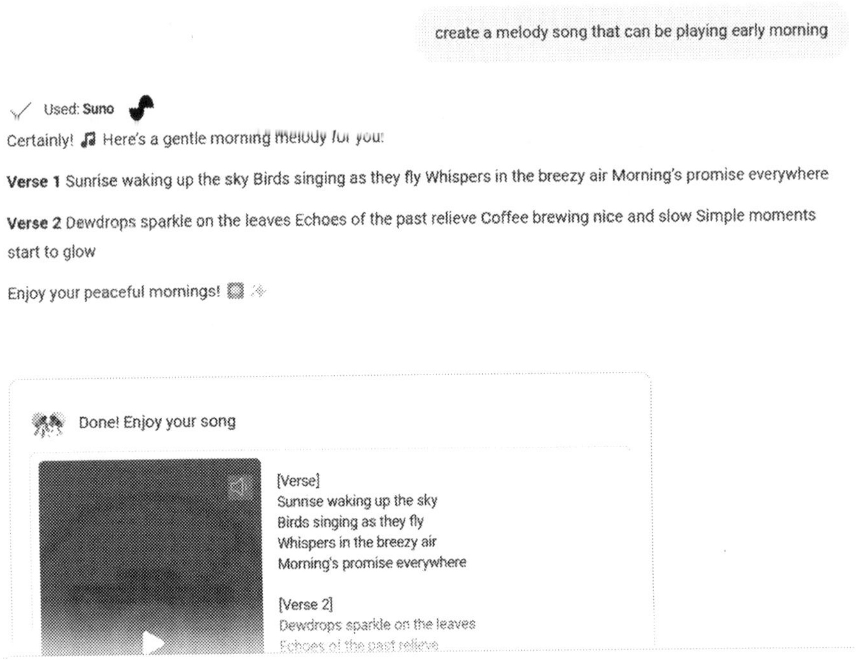

create a melody song that can be playing early morning

√ Used: **Suno** 🎵

Certainly! 🎵 Here's a gentle morning melody for you:

Verse 1 Sunrise waking up the sky Birds singing as they fly Whispers in the breezy air Morning's promise everywhere

Verse 2 Dewdrops sparkle on the leaves Echoes of the past relieve Coffee brewing nice and slow Simple moments start to glow

Enjoy your peaceful mornings! 🎶 ✦

Done! Enjoy your song

[Verse]
Sunrise waking up the sky
Birds singing as they fly
Whispers in the breezy air
Morning's promise everywhere

[Verse 2]
Dewdrops sparkle on the leaves
Echoes of the past relieve

Figure 11-24. *Automate your music talent with Copilot*

Note   Please refer to Chapter 7 for a detailed discussion on Copilot GPTs and plugins.

The Copilot app also enables you to access Notebook. You can provide lengthy prompts to enable Microsoft Copilot to generate a detailed and relevant response. Please refer to Chapter 7 to learn about Copilot Notebook.

Creating Flowcharts

You can create flowcharts easily using Microsoft Copilot. However, Copilot will be able to generate flowcharts in Mermaid format. Mermaid is a Markdown syntax, which generates diagrams from the supplied text. You can generate flowcharts, Unified Modeling Language (UML) diagrams, pie charts, and much more using Mermaid.

The first step is to compile the relevant data and provide a prompt in Copilot as follows:

> *Please create a flowchart using the below items in mermaid format*
>
> *Windows 7 2009*
>
> *Windows 8 2012*
>
> *Windows 10 2015*
>
> *Windows 11 2021*

You can use either Copilot in Windows, the Copilot app, or the Copilot web dashboard. Let's try using the Copilot Windows app. The resulting output looks as shown in Figure 11-25.

Certainly! Here's a flowchart in mermaid format that represents the release timeline of Windows versions:

```
flowchart LR
    W7(Windows 7 - 2009) --> W8(Windows 8 - 2012)
    W8 --> W10(Windows 10 - 2015)
    W10 --> W11(Windows 11 - 2021)
```

You can use this code in any markdown editor that supports mermaid diagrams to visualize the Windows release timeline. Let me know if you need further assistance! 🙂

Figure 11-25. *View the generated Mermaid code*

The next step is to navigate to `https://mermaid.js.org` and select Live Editor located on the top. You should copy and paste the Mermaid format code generated by Copilot. You will see the resulting flowchart as shown in Figure 11-26. The size of the flowchart depends upon the quantity of the data.

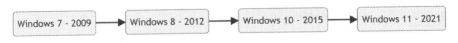

Figure 11-26. Flowchart in action

You can directly copy the code by selecting the Copy icon located inside the generated code. You should note that Microsoft Copilot can be used for advanced programming tasks as well. Moreover, Copilot only generates Mermaid code to create flowcharts. Copilot in Windows 11 can't render flowcharts on its own. You can use the Copilot-generated Mermaid code with plugins like Visual Studio Code, Atom, and Sublime Text as well as the Mermaid.js API and Markdown editors.

Summary

Microsoft Copilot is available as a separate app that can be pinned to the Windows 11 Taskbar. You can easily install the app from the Microsoft Store and explore the functionalities of the Copilot directly via the app. Even if you install the Copilot Windows app, you can work with Copilot via Copilot in Windows (preview), which can be accessed by selecting the Taskbar icon located adjacent to the Notifications icon. You have the option to access Copilot via the Windows 11 Taskbar, desktop, and start menu. The app can also be set to launch automatically upon signing in. Microsoft is continuously improving Copilot, and the ability to access the chatbot as a stand-alone app from within Windows 11 provides enhanced flexibility and productivity. Do you want to learn about the recently announced Copilot key? Jump to the next chapter.

CHAPTER 12

Devices with Copilot Key

Microsoft announced the introduction of a dedicated Copilot key on January 4, 2024. Going forward, new Windows 11 devices such as laptops and convertibles will ship with a new Copilot key depending upon the manufacturer. The integration of the Copilot key represents a significant and intelligent advancement toward the success of future AI-powered PCs. The addition of Copilot in the Windows experience will make it easier for people to take part in the AI transformation. The new Copilot key on the PC keyboard will join the Windows key. If you press the Copilot key as shown in Figure 12-1, you can seamlessly engage with Copilot in your day-to-day activities.

© Anand Narayanaswamy 2024
A. Narayanaswamy, *Microsoft Copilot for Windows 11*, Inside Copilot,
https://doi.org/10.1007/979-8-8688-0583-7_12

Figure 12-1. *Copilot key in action*

The integration of the Copilot key not only simplifies computing productivity but also usability. The Copilot dashboard will open upon pressing the Copilot key without any need to click the Windows 11 Taskbar icon. You also need not have to press the WIN+C keyboard shortcut. However, if Copilot is not available in your region, then Windows Search will open upon hitting the Copilot key.

Note   Microsoft integrated the Windows key to PC keyboards in 1994 along with the launch of the natural keyboard. Gateway Solo was the first laptop to ship with the Windows key.

The new Copilot key will change the way we adopt technology across work and life. Microsoft announced that Intel, AMD, and Qualcomm have already introduced new silicon innovations via exclusive chipsets, which unlock new AI experiences while computing. The core purpose is to bring the power of CPU, GPU, NPU, and cloud architecture under a single umbrella for an intuitive AI experience. Devices with the Copilot key that are manufactured by Samsung, ASUS, Acer, and Lenovo were showcased during the CES 2024 and MWC 2024 conferences. In this chapter, you will learn about the list of Windows 11 devices that ships with the Copilot key.

> **Caution**   Even though the devices mentioned in this chapter were released with the Copilot key, the features and specifications are subject to change without notice. Moreover, the availability of Microsoft Copilot varies depending on the region. Refer to the product link and manufacturer's website for price-related information.

Microsoft Surface Laptop 6

Microsoft Surface Laptop 6 is available in both 13.5-inch and 15-inch PixelSense displays. The Surface Laptop 6 is also named AI PC for Business and is not available for end consumers. You can opt for either Intel Core Ultra 5 Processor 135H or Intel Core Ultra 7 Processor 165H variants, respectively, with Intel AI Boost technology and Intel Arc Graphics. The devices are available in 8GB, 16GB, 32GB, and 64GB RAM variants with up to 1TB storage. Microsoft has integrated the Trusted Platform Module (TPM) 2.0 chip for enhanced security with support for BitLocker and Windows Hello technologies. The laptop offers an FHD Surface Studio camera alongside Windows Studio Effects. The audio is powered via Omnisonic Speakers with Dolby Atmos technology and Bluetooth LE Audio support. The laptop is manufactured using MIL-STD 810H standards, which is resistant to temperature, dust, and vibration. The device is exclusively designed to balance power and performance with an extended battery life with 80% charging in less than 60 minutes.

Note `www.microsoft.com/en-in/surface/business/`
`surface-laptop-6`

Samsung Galaxy Book4

Samsung Galaxy Book4 features a 15.6-inch anti-glare display coupled with 512GB storage. The laptop is available in Intel Core 7 150U and Intel Core 5 120U processor variants. The laptop includes all the standard connectivity ports and is preloaded with Windows 11. The US version of the Samsung Galaxy Book4 series includes a dedicated Copilot key. The laptop is designed to provide intelligent performance, improved security, and an interactive display enclosed in an ultra-portable form factor. Moreover, if you work with a Samsung Galaxy smartphone, then you will be able to establish connectivity with the Galaxy Book4 via Microsoft Copilot.

Note `www.samsung.com/us/computing/galaxy-books/`
`galaxy-book4-series/`

Acer Aspire 3D 15 SpatialLabs Edition

Acer Aspire 3D 15 SpatialLabs Edition features a 15.6-inch 4K UHD display, 13th Gen Intel Core i7 processor alongside NVIDIA GeForce RTX 4050 Laptop GPU. The device provides a true cinematic experience through an immersive 3D rendering with the help of a specialized optical lens and eye-tracking technology. The laptop leverages stereoscopic 3D technology and works with exceptional speed, which is perfect for powerful computing tasks and gaming. Some of the other features of the device are Acer PurifiedView and Acer PurifiedVoice AI Noise Reduction. The addition of dual fans and triple copper heat pipes dissipate heat efficiently and provide reliable thermal management. The laptop includes Wi-Fi 6, USB Type-C, and HDMI 2.1 ports.

Note   www.acer.com/in-en/laptops/aspire/aspire-3d-15-spatiallabs-edition

Acer Aspire Vero 16

Acer Aspire Vero 16 is equipped with a 16-inch display and is available in both touch and non-touch displays. You can work seamlessly because of 16GB RAM and up to 1TB SSD storage. The display covers 100% of sRGB color space and is a great choice not only for work but also for entertainment purposes. The laptop is integrated with an Intel Core Ultra 7 processor coupled with Intel AI Boost and MIL-STD-810H military-grade durability. The system is capable of delivering up to 10.5 hours of battery life on a single charge via USB-C fast charging technology. Acer has integrated flagship PurifiedView and PurifiedVoice AI technologies in addition to AcerSense app to provide an enhanced user experience. Moreover, the laptop is EPEAT Gold certified and has adopted 200% recycled packaging and an ocean-bound plastic touchpad.

Note   www.acer.com/us-en/laptops/aspire/aspire-vero-16

Acer Swift Go 16

Acer Swift Go 16 features a 16-inch ultra-smooth 120Hz OLED Eyesafe Certified 2.0 display paired with an Intel Core Ultra 9 processor and Intel Arc graphics. The system offers up to 32GB RAM and 2TB SSD storage, respectively, with XeSS AI-enhanced upscaling, Xe media engine, and Intel AI boost capabilities. The laptop is designed to offer up to 10.5 hours of battery life, which is sufficient for all work, including Copilot-related tasks. You will experience seamless interaction across multiple devices via Intel Unison. The other features of Swift Go 16 are Acer PurifiedView, Acer PurifiedVoice, and 1440p QHD webcam. The overall user experience can be customized with the AcerSense app. The laptop is designed using a light aluminum body with a fully extendable hinge. Acer Swift Go 14 features a 14-inch display, 16GB RAM, and 512GB SSD storage alongside Intel Xe graphics technology. The laptop ships with an Intel Core i5 processor and includes a dedicated Copilot key. The remaining features are the same as the Acer Swift Go 16.

Note   www.acer.com/in-en/laptops/swift/swift-go-16

Acer Predator Helios 18

Acer Predator Helios 18 boasts a massive 18-inch neon display. The 250Hz refresh rate alongside 1000-nits brightness delivers an immersive gaming experience. The laptop is powered by the 14th Gen Intel Core processor with 32GB RAM. The integration of NVIDIA GeForce RTX 4090 graphics processor, NVidia DLSS 3.5, and Ray Tracing delivers brilliant AI-enabled graphics with additional high-quality frames.

You will be able to customize clicks and keys with the help of MagClick and MagSpeed. Acer has integrated dual 5th Gen AeroBlade 3D fans with liquid metal thermal grease to ensure maximum performance during intense gaming. You will experience improved connectivity with Wi-Fi 7 technology, which ensures uninterrupted and secured AR, VR, and 8K streaming. In addition to PurifiedVoice 2.0, the laptop ships preloaded with Adobe Creative Cloud suite, Blender, Blackmagic Davinci Resolve, OBS Studio, NVIDIA Omniverse, Adobe Substance, Adobe Painter, Blender, Unreal Engine, and much more.

Note   www.acer.com/in-en/predator/laptops/helios/
helios-18

ASUS ProArt P16

ASUS ProArt P16 is equipped with a 4K (3840 × 2400) OLED SGS Eye Care touch display, AMD Ryzen AI 9 HX 370 Processor, 64GB RAM, and 2TB storage alongside NVIDIA GeForce RTX 4070 graphics processor. The laptop has been designed using US MIL-STD 810H military-grade standard and provides support for Windows Hello. The entertainment segment is amplified with Smart Amp technology, which eliminates studio-quality sound. The device provides support for Wi-Fi 7 and Bluetooth 5.4 and includes all the essential ports with a Backlit Chiclet Keyboard.

Note   www.asus.com/laptops/for-creators/proart/
proart-p16-h7606/

ASUS ProArt PX13

ASUS ProArt PX13 carries a 13.3-inch 3K OLED Eye Care touch display, AMD Ryzen AI 9 HX 370 Processor, XDNA up to 50 TOPS neural processor, 32GB RAM, and 1TB storage. The laptop is designed using US MIL-STD 810H military-grade standard technology alongside NVIDIA GeForce RTX 4060 graphics processor. The device includes a Backlit Chiclet Keyboard with support for Windows Hello and Smart Amp technologies. The company has termed the laptop as an AI Studio PC because of its exceptional performance and power-saving capabilities.

Note   www.asus.com/laptops/for-creators/proart/proart-px13-hn7306/

ASUS Zenbook S 16

ASUS Zenbook S 16 features 3K OLED 16:10 SGS Eye Care touch display, AMD Ryzen AI 9 HX 370/AMD Ryzen AI 9 365 Processors, AMD Radeon 880M/890M graphics chipset, 24GB/32GB RAM, and 1TB storage. The device also includes XDNA up to 50TOPs neural processor, which amplifies AI performance. ASUS has integrated Wi-Fi 7, Bluetooth 5.4, Windows Hello, and Smart Amp technologies in addition to standard connectivity ports. The system is available in both Windows 11 Home/Pro variants.

Note   www.asus.com/laptops/for-home/zenbook/asus-zenbook-s-16-um5606/

Lenovo Legion 7i

The Lenovo Legion 7i laptop is available in two display models such as a 3.2K 100% DCI-P3 and a traditional WQXGA (2560 × 1600) with 250Hz refresh rate. The laptop is powered by an Intel Core i9-14900HX processor, up to 32GB RAM, and an NVIDIA GeForce RTX 4070 graphics processor. The addition of Legion ColdFront Hyper with dual fans spinning in opposite directions provides enhanced cooling capabilities. The full-sized Legion TrueStrike gaming keyboard with a large Mylar touchpad and FHD camera with a privacy shutter ensures an extended trouble-free computing experience. Lenovo claims that the device can be charged completely in 80 minutes via 140W USB-C Super Rapid Charge technology. The entertainment is power-packed with Nahimic Audio by SteelSeries technology.

Dell Latitude 7350 Detachable

Dell Latitude 7350 Detachable is a convertible laptop, which ships with an additional keyboard with a dedicated Copilot key. The device offers a 3K ComfortView Plus Corning Gorilla Glass Victus display with 500-nits brightness. The display substantially reduces blue light emissions without sacrificing color quality. Dell Latitude 7350 is powered by Intel Core Ultra 5 134U, 16GB RAM, and 512GB SSD storage preloaded with Windows 11 Pro. The 8MP HDR IR front camera with smart privacy features is well supported by an 8MP rear camera.

Tecno Megabook T16

Tecno Mobile has announced the release of the Megabook T16 2024 laptop with AI power. The laptop is integrated with a 16-inch FHD Lande Eye Comfort expanded horizon display, 13th Gen Intel Core i5 Processor,

16GB RAM, and 512GB/1TB storage. The device ships with enhanced cooling performance with support for AI Conference and AI ENC technologies. The system delivers intelligent audio performance with DTS X Ultra surround sound technology. The addition of WiFi 6 ensures 200m ultra-long-range connections with 50% file transfer speed. The laptop includes a backlit numeric keyboard and an oversized trackpad coupled with nine ports. Like in the case of previous Megabook counterparts, the fingerprint sensor is integrated into the power button. In addition to the Megabook T16 laptop, the company announced the features of the Megabook T16 Pro laptop on its official website. However, Tecno is yet to reveal the pricing or launch date.

Note   www.tecno-mobile.com/laptops/product-list

Summary

In this chapter, you have learned the features and specifications of the devices with the Copilot key in a nutshell. If you purchase a device with a Copilot key, you can activate the AI chatbot just by pressing the key. You can then interact with Copilot by providing text and image prompts. You can also ask Copilot in Windows to generate images. Going forward, you can expect more manufacturers to ship devices with the Copilot key. We expect that all laptops will ship with a dedicated Copilot key within two years. Moreover, third-party manufacturers have started to release external keyboards with the Copilot key. The newly launched HP 480 Comfort Wired Keyboard ships with a dedicated Copilot key. Adesso also launched several PC keyboards with the Copilot key. In the next chapter, we will examine the list of trending devices that are tagged as Copilot+ PCs.

CHAPTER 13

Introducing Copilot+ PCs

Microsoft announced the launch of Copilot+ PCs on May 20, 2024, during the sidelines of the Microsoft Build conference. Copilot+ PCs are designed to deliver a robust user experience with the help of Recall, Live Captions, Paint Cocreator, and Windows Studio Effects. Copilot+ PCs are designed to provide next-level AI experience with enhanced security, speed, and personalization. As of this writing, Copilot+ PCs are powered by Snapdragon X series processors. Microsoft revealed that Intel and AMD will also launch exclusive chipsets for Copilot+ PCs in the upcoming months. Microsoft, ASUS, Samsung, HP, and Dell have released Copilot+ PCs with powerful features with general availability from June 18, 2024. In this chapter, you will learn about the new devices that are tagged as Copilot+ PCs.

Launch Video   www.youtube.com/watch?v=aZbHd4suAnQ

© Anand Narayanaswamy 2024
A. Narayanaswamy, *Microsoft Copilot for Windows 11*, Inside Copilot,
https://doi.org/10.1007/979-8-8688-0583-7_13

Microsoft Surface Laptop 7

Microsoft released the Surface Laptop 7 in both 13.8-inch and 15-inch Pixelsense Flow display variants. The laptop is powered by Snapdragon X Plus/Elite processor variants, Hexagon Neural Processing Unit (NPU) with 45 Trillion Operations Per Second (TOPS), and Adreno graphics. The device is available in 16GB/32GB RAM variants with 256GB/512GB and 1TB storage capacities. You have a choice to pick a configuration as per your requirements. The minimum requirement for a Copilot+ PC device is 40 TOPS NPU, 16GB RAM, and 256GB of storage. The laptop also includes advanced security features such as Microsoft Pluton TPM 2.0, Windows Hello, and Windows Defender. Microsoft has integrated Omnisonic Speakers with Dolby Atmos technology and Bluetooth LE. The Surface Studio Camera provides an immersive video calling experience.

Note www.microsoft.com/en-in/surface/devices/surface-laptop-7th-edition

---

Microsoft Surface Pro 11

Microsoft Surface Pro 11 is a convertible Copilot+ PC powered by both Snapdragon X Plus and X Elite processors. While the X Elite variant is integrated with an OLED display, the X Plus model offers a traditional LCD. The laptop includes a 13-inch PixelSense Flow display, Qualcomm Hexagon with 45 TOPS, and Adreno graphics. The device is integrated with 16GB/32GB RAM coupled with 256GB, 512GB, and 1TB storage capacities. The addition of the 1440p Quad HD Surface Studio Camera delivers a brilliant video calling experience well supported by a 10MP rear camera. The product is bundled with a 165-degree hinge kickstand with dual speakers. The system borrows all the core security functionalities of Surface Laptop 7.

Note   www.microsoft.com/en-in/surface/devices/
surface-pro-11th-edition

ASUS ProArt PZ13

ASUS ProArt PZ13 features a 13-inch OLED 120Hz touch detachable display, Snapdragon X Series processor, 70Wh battery, and dual cameras coupled with 45 TOPS NPU. The Copilot+ PC device is designed to provide a seamless working experience without sacrificing battery life and is available with up to 16GB RAM and 1TB storage capacities. The laptop includes the exclusive StoryCube app, which is an AI-enabled media hub and is preloaded with Windows 11 Home. The bundled ASUS Pen 2.0 provides 4096 pressure levels with a 266Hz sampling rate. The IP52 rating and the addition of military-grade materials enable the laptop to work under extreme sunlight and even freezing temperatures. Moreover, it can resist solar radiation, temperature shock, and vibration. The system ships with a detachable keyboard and the required I/O ports.

Note   www.asus.com/us/laptops/for-creators/proart/
proart-pz13-ht5306/

ASUS Vivobook S15

ASUS Vivobook S15 flaunts a 15.6-inch 3K 120Hz ASUS Lumina OLED display, Snapdragon X Elite processor, Adreno graphics, 16GB RAM, and 1TB storage. The laptop is manufactured using premium all-metal thin and light form factor with an immersive audio system. The system is powered by a 12-core chipset with Qualcomm AI Engine up to 45 TOPS NPU for instant AI rendering. The customizable and ergonomic single-zone RGB keyboard provides an exciting typing experience. The 70Wh battery is integrated into the system, which is capable of delivering 18 hours of battery life. In addition to standard connectivity ports, the laptop also ships with ASUS AI noise-cancelling technology with machine learning support. The MIL-STD 810H military standard technology integrated into the Copilot+ PC ensures enhanced reliability and durability.

> **Note** www.asus.com/in/laptops/for-home/vivobook/
> asus-vivobook-s-15-s5507

Samsung Galaxy Book4 Edge

Samsung Galaxy Book4 Edge is available in both 14-inch and 16-inch 3K Dynamic AMOLED touch displays. The system is powered by dual variants of Snapdragon X Elite processor along with Adreno graphics. While the system memory is 16GB, you have a choice to select 512GB or 1TB storage model. In addition to the latest Wi-Fi 7, the laptop ships with all major connectivity ports. The entertainment segment is amplified with AKG Quad Speakers enabled with Dolby Atmos technology.

> **Note** www.samsung.com/us/computing/galaxy-books/
> galaxy-book4-edge/

Lenovo Yoga Slim 7x

Lenovo Yoga Slim 7x is equipped with a 14.5-inch 3K 90Hz 1000-nits PureSight OLED touch display, Snapdragon X Elite chipset, Adreno graphics, and up to 32GB RAM and 1TB storage. The eco-friendly laptop includes four Dolby Atmos speakers and microphones. Lenovo has applied military standard technology to ensure extreme durability. The 70Whr battery enables you to work for an extended time by leveraging Lenovo AI Core. The laptop is bundled with Adobe Creative Cloud membership.

Note `www.lenovo.com/us/en/laptops/`

HP OmniBook X

HP also entered the Copilot+ PC bandwagon with the launch of OmniBook X. The laptop boasts a 14-inch IPS display, Snapdragon X Elite processor, Adreno graphics, Hexagon NPU, 16GB RAM, and 1TB storage. The device is capable of charging 50% within 30 minutes via an AI-enabled battery. The premium recycled aluminum construction shines in your office space.

Note `www.hp.com/in-en/shop/hp-omnibook-x-laptop-14-fe0121qu-a99b8pa.html`

Dell XPS 13 9345

Dell XPS 13 9345 features a 13.4-inch FHD+ EyeSafe InfinityEdge display in addition to QHD+ and OLED display variants. You can opt for either a 16GB, 32GB, or 64GB RAM variant. Moreover, the storage option is available up to 2TB with 512GB being the default capacity. The device is powered by a Snapdragon X Elite chipset and Adreno graphics processor. The addition of Hexagon NPU with 45 TOPS emits less heat and extends battery life to a large extent. The device provides support for dual Type-C ports, Wi-Fi 7, and an FHD camera. The laptop also includes a precision touchpad with haptic functionality in addition to a dedicated camera. The laptop is designed using CNC aluminum material for improved durability.

Note www.dell.com/en-us/shop/dell-laptops/xps-13-laptop/spd/xps-13-9345-laptop

Dell Inspiron 14 Plus

Dell Inspiron 14 Plus is equipped with a 14-inch QHD+ 400-nits IPS display alongside an integrated Snapdragon X Plus processor and Adreno graphics processor. The system offers 16GB RAM and 512GB storage with support for FHD camera. Additionally, the laptop is available with a Snapdragon X Elite processor and 1TB of storage. The system is bundled with a stereo speaker with Qualcomm Aqstic Speaker Max technology and dual 2W woofer and tweeters. The aluminum finish provides a premium decor to your home and workplace.

Note www.dell.com/en-us/shop/dell-laptops/inspiron-14-plus-laptop/spd/inspiron-14-7441-laptop

Summary

Copilot+ PCs can change the way you engage with computers at both home and work. The devices are shipped with powerful specifications such as 16GB RAM by default and up to 1TB storage, including powerful audio capabilities. You can quickly complete all the required tasks, including gaming with these devices. These devices are preloaded with exclusive Windows 11 features such as Recall, Windows Studio Effects, and Live Captions that can take your computing experience to the next level. Going forward, you can expect the launch of new Copilot+ PCs with exciting features and specifications. AI has been put to use in all sectors such as technology, mobile, education, healthcare, and much more. Microsoft Copilot can be used as a valuable tool for education since it can solve all problems you throw in. Microsoft is investing heavily in AI both in terms of hardware and software. We foresee a great future for Copilot+ PCs, and many more companies will foray into the manufacturing of these devices. You will probably visit the nearest electronics retail shop after two years only to find Copilot+ PCs. The future is AI, and you can expect great developments in this field in the future.

APPENDIX A

Glossary

There are several terms associated with AI. However, it's difficult to locate them since they are scattered all over the Web. In this appendix, you will learn about the important terms in addition to useful tools that are related to AI in a digest format.

Algorithm

An algorithm is a series of rules that are provided to an AI model. This will help the system to perform the corresponding task or to solve a particular problem.

Artificial Intelligence

Artificial intelligence (AI) is a subfield of computer science, which focuses on the creation of intelligent machines that can learn from vast amounts of data. The system immediately reacts upon user input, also called a prompt. OpenAI, Microsoft, and Google have created their own AI platforms to enable people to interact effectively to enhance productivity and creativity. Moreover, chatbots can generate various types of content.

Big Data

Big data refers to massive, large, and complex datasets that are primarily used to study trends that will support business decisions. The collected data can be analyzed using special tools.

© Anand Narayanaswamy 2024
A. Narayanaswamy, *Microsoft Copilot for Windows 11*, Inside Copilot,
https://doi.org/10.1007/979-8-8688-0583-7

Chatbot

A chatbot is a software app that borrows the intelligence of humans while rendering responses via both text and images. If you work with ChatGPT or Copilot, then it implies that you are interacting with a chatbot.

ChatGPT

ChatGPT (`https://chatgpt.com`) is a Generative AI chatbot launched on November 30, 2022, developed by OpenAI. The system uses natural language processing technology, which makes use of machine learning and deep learning technologies to deliver results based on user queries. The launch of ChatGPT has shaken the tech industry. This prompted other companies to speed up the development of similar systems.

Claude

Claude (`https://claude.ai`) is a Generative AI chatbot developed by Anthropic. The recently released Claude 3.5 Sonnet chatbot includes advanced intelligent features. It's said to beat competitors and also the previous counterpart of Claude, which is Opus. Like in the case of Copilot, Claude is available in both free and paid versions.

Copilot Key

The Copilot key is a dedicated key on the keyboard, which when pressed opens Copilot in Windows. Microsoft introduced the key on January 4, 2024. Microsoft and other manufacturers have started to release new devices with the Copilot key.

Copilot+ PCs

Copilot+ PCs are advanced devices integrated with a dedicated central processing unit (CPU) and neural processing unit (NPU) along with a companion graphics chipset. The devices are currently being released with Qualcomm Snapdragon X series processors with the possibility of Intel and AMD jumping into the AI bandwagon by Q4 2024. Microsoft has announced new features such as Recall, Live Captions, and Windows Studio Effects that will ship with the Copilot+ PCs. You should note that AI is processed locally in Copilot+ PCs.

CriticGPT

CriticGPT is a new GPT-4 model launched by OpenAI to address bugs and errors in code generated by ChatGPT. The system has been integrated into OpenAI's Reinforcement Learning from Human Feedback (RLHF) to provide the required tools for AI trainers. OpenAI announced the launch of SearchGPT on July 25, 2024. The search User Interface will be enriched with advanced AI capabilities to provide accurate answers with relevant sources.

DALL·E

Dall·E is the text-to-image model developed by OpenAI using deep learning technologies. The model generates images from natural language texts, also called prompts. OpenAI released the first version in January 2021 followed by several new iterations. While Microsoft has integrated DALL·E 3 into Copilot, the same model is available for consumption via ChatGPT Plus and Enterprise plans.

Deep Learning

Deep learning is a type of machine learning that makes use of artificial multilayered neural networks, which simulate the complex structure of the human brain. This comprises text, images, and speech that are typically used by AI apps and chatbots.

Gemini

Gemini (`https://gemini.google.com`), launched by Google, is a powerful multimodal Large Language Model developed to serve as the successor to the LaMDA and PaLM 2 models. Google launched the Gemini chatbot (same name as the model) on December 6, 2023, which comprises Gemini Ultra, Gemini Pro, and Gemini Nano. The company has termed Gemini as a powerful competitor to the GPT model. Google also launched the Gemini Advanced paid subscription package with access to the Gemini

1.0 Ultra model in addition to advanced performance and other perks. Gemini is capable of delivering responses based on both text and image prompts. Google Gemini is also capable of extracting information from Google Workspace, YouTube, YouTube Music, and Google Maps. You can invoke @gmail, @docs, @youtube, etc., to fetch information. For example, you can ask Gemini to fetch all emails with a particular ID or a song from YouTube.

GPT

GPT, also called generative pre-trained transformer, is a model architecture employed by AI chatbots like ChatGPT and Microsoft Copilot. These models are trained aggressively in a large number of datasets. The Copilot Pro subscription enables you to work with GPT-4 Turbo, which is more powerful than GPT-4. The latest model GPT-4o is capable of generating responses in text, image, and video formats, respectively. The reports as of July 2024 indicate that the GPT-5 is expected to be released in 2025 and will ship with PhD-level intelligence.

Grok

Grok is a Generative AI chatbot developed by xAI. You can access Grok from within X (formerly Twitter) after purchasing a suitable plan. Unlike other AI chatbots, Grok is not a free product. Grok has been developed in such a way as to provide responses that have a sense of humor.

Krutrim

Krutrim (`https://chat.olakrutrim.com`), developed by India-based Ola, is an AI chatbot using which you can create, learn, and discover facts.

Leonardo

Leonardo (`https://leonardo.ai`) enables you to generate impressive production-quality AI images with the help of advanced tools. Moreover, the recently launched Leonardo Phoenix helps you to work with the most advanced model. You can configure presets, style, contrasts, generation mode, and dimensions from the dashboard. The paid plan provides faster image generation and additional tokens. Leonardo accepts prompts that run several sentences.

LLaMA

LLaMA, also called Large Language Model Meta AI, is a Generative AI model released by Meta on February 24, 2023. It's used by the company to power Meta AI on WhatsApp and Instagram. The latest stable release is Llama 3 which is capable of performing all tasks, including generating code using natural language prompts. The model can also generate images based on prompts.

LLM

A Large Language Model (LLM) is a type of AI program that can understand and generate human language. LLMs are trained on an enormous quantity of text content, which could be from books, articles, websites, blogs, and code. You can note that the entire data which is available on the Internet can be indexed. The purpose of the training is to enable them to better understand language and emit human-generated content. The technology behind LLMs is a type of neural network called a transformer. You should note that AI chatbots like Copilot and Gemini are part of LLM.

Lunar Lake

Lunar Lake is the name for the next-generation AI-enabled chipsets from Intel. The Lunar Lake processors feature enhanced performance and efficiency over the previous counterparts. The chipsets are expected to ship with a 48 TOPS NPU on top of 67 TOPS GPU. Even though the chipset offers all basic connectivity options, the memory will be bundled with the processor with no option for upgradeability.

Metis

Metis is the rumored codename for the upcoming Generative AI
project being developed by Amazon. The chatbot will be powered by
Amazon's Olympus model.

Midjourney

Midjourney (www.midjourney.com) is a popular Generative AI-based
image generation platform launched on July 12, 2022. The platform
generates stunning images from natural language prompts. You can create
images using Discord bot commands. Midjourney is currently available
for free with 25 image credits per user. However, the company reserves the
right to remove the free trial without notice. The purpose of the free trial is
to help users experience the powerful capabilities of the AI imaging tool.

ML

Machine learning (ML) is a field of AI in which specific algorithms
are deployed to enhance the performance of tasks via rigorous data
analysis. The required training is devised to teach machines to learn from
the patterns and then apply them to make decisions. This technology
makes use of large chunks of datasets. The end result is the evolution of AI
systems and chatbots, such as ChatGPT, Copilot, and Gemini.

MLOps

Machine learning operations (MLOps) are designed to automate and
simplify machine learning workflows. The combination of ML and AI can
solve real-world problems effectively.

NLP

Natural language processing (NLP) mainly focuses on the
collaboration between computers and human languages. NLP is a
technology employed in the development of AI systems. Moreover, they
can read and analyze large loads of unstructured data content.

NPU

The neural processing unit (NPU) is a type of processor designed to efficiently handle machine learning tasks. The work done by NPUs often involves operations on large multidimensional arrays. The NPU is designed to process large chunks of data and can perform trillions of operations per second. The devices with NPU chipsets consume less power and perform high-bandwidth AI tasks when compared with a traditional CPU or GPU. You will find devices with NPU useful during the generation of images and usage of voice-enabled apps.

Perplexity

Perplexity (`www.perplexity.ai`) is an AI-enabled search engine, which works by leveraging Multiple Large Language Models (LLMs). This includes GPT-4 and Claude 3 as well as custom models to deliver accurate and context-relevant answers.

Poe

Poe (`https://poe.com`) is a free AI chatbot developed by Quora. You can access advanced bots and models under one single umbrella. This includes ChatGPT, GPT-4o, DALL·E 3, Claude 3 Opus, and Claude 3.5 Sonnet, among others. The paid version enables you to work without any limits and credits.

Prompt

The query that you provide inside an AI chatbot such as Copilot is called a prompt. It could be either a text or an image query based on which the chatbot delivers the response. For example, if you ask Microsoft Copilot with a query like *write Hello World program in C++*, then this request is called a prompt. You should make sure to use efficient prompts. This is because a good prompt delivers a good output. You will improve the art of writing good prompts if you continuously work with Copilot.

Prompt Engineering

If you work with Generative AI tools, then you need to know about the art of providing user requests to the chatbot to retrieve proper responses. This area of study is called prompt engineering. The more accurate your prompt is, the better the chatbot responds to you. You will learn the nuances of writing a good prompt only upon experience. Your prompt should look in such a way that it should not harm the AI ecosystem. Moreover, you should make use of the image generation system responsibly and avoid manipulation to avoid being caught by law enforcement agencies.

Sora

OpenAI announced the Sora model (`https://openai.com/index/sora`) on February 15, 2024. The main functionality of Sora is its ability to create videos from text prompts. The company demonstrated the capabilities of Sora and also previewed multiple clips of HD videos. These include an SUV driving down a mountain road and much more. The model is designed to generate realistic and stunning videos up to one minute based on the text instructions. As of this writing, Sora is available only to a select group of people. The system will be refined based on the user's feedback.

Snapdragon X Elite

Snapdragon X Elite is a powerful and intelligent processor designed by Qualcomm for Windows devices. These processors are embedded with Qualcomm Hexagon NPU with 45 TOPS. The devices powered by this processor deliver excellent productivity and creativity.

Supervised Learning

In the supervised machine learning algorithm, the training data includes not only labeled data input but also the desired output, also called the response.

TOPS

The trillions of operations per second (TOPS) is a way to measure the performance of AI processors. Technically, TOPS is calculated based on the architecture and frequency of the processor such as NPU. This term is commonly referred to in conjunction with the Copilot+ PC specifications. The devices recently released by Microsoft and other manufacturers are based on Qualcomm Hexagon NPU with 45 TOPS.

Unsupervised Learning

The system uses unlabeled data while working with unsupervised learning. The AI platform automatically locates the hidden patterns or structures within the data.

Windows Insiders

Windows Insiders (`www.microsoft.com/windowsinsider`) are a group of professionals and tech enthusiasts who actively provide feedback after testing new versions/builds of Windows. Microsoft has created channels such as Dev, Canary, Beta, and Release Preview through which new builds are pushed regularly. The advantage of becoming a Windows Insider is that users can test new features before they are made available to the general public.

APPENDIX B

Additional Resources

Copilot Lab

https://copilot.cloud.microsoft/en-US/prompts

Microsoft Learn Copilot Learning Hub

https://learn.microsoft.com/en-us/copilot

Get Started with Copilot for Microsoft 365

https://learn.microsoft.com/en-us/training/paths/
get-started-with-microsoft-365-copilot

Microsoft Copilot Success Kit

https://adoption.microsoft.com/en-us/copilot/success-kit

Copilot for Microsoft 365 for Administrators Course

https://learn.microsoft.com/en-us/training/courses/ms-4006

Microsoft Copilot LinkedIn Training

www.linkedin.com/learning/topics/copilot

Microsoft Copilot Social Media

https://twitter.com/MSFTCopilot

www.instagram.com/microsoftcopilot

Windows

www.microsoft.com/en-us/windows

© Anand Narayanaswamy 2024
A. Narayanaswamy, *Microsoft Copilot for Windows 11*, Inside Copilot,
https://doi.org/10.1007/979-8-8688-0583-7

Blogs

Microsoft Copilot: www.microsoft.com/microsoft-copilot/blog
   Microsoft: https://blogs.microsoft.com
   Microsoft 365: www.microsoft.com/en-us/microsoft-365/blog
   Windows: https://blogs.windows.com

YouTube

Microsoft: www.youtube.com/@Microsoft
   Windows: www.youtube.com/@MicrosoftWindows

Index

© Anand Narayanaswamy 2024
A. Narayanaswamy, *Microsoft Copilot for Windows 11*, Inside Copilot,
https://doi.org/10.1007/979-8-8688-0583-7

Printed in the United States
by Baker & Taylor Publisher Services